AN INTRODUCTION TO
JEWISH BIBLE COMMENTARY

AN INTRODUCTION TO

JEWISH
BIBLE COMMENTARY

by

BERNARD M. CASPER

Rabbi, Dean of Students
The Hebrew University, Jerusalem

NEW YORK   THOMAS YOSELOFF   LONDON

Prepared under the editorial direction of
The World Jewish Congress, British Section

Published by
Thomas Yoseloff, New York and London

Made and Printed in Great Britain by
Fletcher and Son Ltd Norwich and
The Leighton-Straker Bookbinding Co Ltd London

Contents

Note: The index numbers used in the body of the text refer to the list of Hebrew Quotations given at the end of the book in APPENDIX A.

Preface

WHILE there are a great number of books, in the English language, on Jewish history, the ordinary lay reader has to search hard for information concerning the development of Biblical exegesis. Yet this is a most important aspect of Jewish history; for battles, persecutions and expulsions, together with their dates, are but the material framework in the setting of which one sees the uninterrupted and abiding devotion of the people to its spiritual treasures. None of the tragic events that mark the story of our people since Biblical times, shattering as some of them appear in the context of social existence, has ever succeeded in deflecting Israel's attention from the study and interpretation of the Torah. Whether in Babylonian captivity or under the tyranny of Roman procurators, in the shadow of national exile and destruction or against the impact of Christianity or Islam—at all times the main preoccupation was the preservation and transmission of the Holy Scriptures. It is in the study of all this labour of love that we see the long spiritual odyssey of the Jewish people.

The present volume is not intended for the learned scholar in the field of Jewish studies. Its purpose is to put into the hand of the layman, in concise form, a guide to a selected few of the giants who contributed to the elucidation of the Bible and an indication of their respective methods and styles, as well as a glance at the times in which they lived— the background to their life and work. Some of the actors in this story were magnificent figures who walked the stage of history with a dignified grandeur and a picturesque, romantic bearing, like Abravanel or Ibn Ezra; others, like the

Massoretes, remained anonymous. But all left their mark; and in their respective and varied contributions it is possible to detect not only a historic continuity, but a unity of purpose and approach. For each and every one saw his task as essentially a religious task—the search for the true meaning of the Word of God. In their work we see the gradual extension of that long chain of tradition which is a part of the Oral Law whose roots are as ancient as the text of the Written Torah itself. The knowledge of their lives and teachings is thus of special significance for the understanding of historic Judaism.

I am grateful to Mr. Desmond J. Trenner for having read both the typescript of the text and the proofs, and for his many helpful suggestions. I express my thanks also to the World Jewish Congress (British Section) for including the book in the distinguished company of the volumes already forming its *Popular Jewish Library*.

Jerusalem 5720–1960   B.M.C.

1

Commentary in Scripture

NOT FOR nothing has the Jewish people come to be called the 'People of the Book'. Throughout its history, no aspect of life or thought has so occupied its attention or commanded its loving care as the understanding of the Bible. The proper understanding of the text and teachings of Scripture has always been the most popular and assiduously cultivated occupation of the Jewish mind. In the first thousand years of its history, the people of Israel was concerned chiefly with the compilation of the Books of the Bible; and from then on (i.e. from the days of Ezra in the fifth century B.C.E.), right up to the present day, its main literary preoccupation has been with the exposition and interpretation of those Books. Thus the best part of a second thousand years was devoted to the systematic development of the law, or *Halacha*, to be deduced from the Biblical text, as well as to the *Aggada*, that is, the non-legal interpretations comprising what may be termed folklore, homilies, moral narratives and anecdotes, and similar subjects. The *Halacha* and the *Aggada* are the two component elements of the old Rabbinic literature and cover the period of the *Tannaim* (the teachers of the Mishna, up to about 200 C.E.) and the *Amoraim*—the makers of the Talmud for another three centuries in the centres of both Palestine and Babylon. In the same way, the Hellenistic literature of the Jews of the Greek period, evidenced particularly in the allegorical interpretations of Philo; even the work of the Jewish historian of Roman times, Josephus, the first part of his *Antiquities* being a running commentary on the narrative portions of the Bible; and certainly the literature of the Rabbanite-Karaite controversy of the ninth and tenth centuries; as well as the Jewish philosophical works of the Middle Ages, produced largely under the challenge of Islam and Christianity; and, on the other hand, the Kabbala and subsequent manifestations of Jewish mysticism;—all were largely based upon, and often written in the form of commentary on the Biblical text. The importance with which Jews always viewed the proper interpretation of Holy Scripture is matched by the enormous volume of commentary-literature produced through the centuries. A detailed and schematic history of all this literature would be a most formidable task; the purpose of the present volume is merely to sketch in briefest outline the lives and contributions of some of those who have been most influential in shaping our understanding of the Book of Books.

The formal story goes back to the early days of the Second Temple. The Jews who had returned to Judea from Babylon soon came upon hard times; drought, famine, loneliness, attacks from hostile neighbours—all contributed to produce a general demoralisation within the small community. Hearing of these difficulties, Ezra, a scribe in Babylon, went to Judea with authority vested in him by the Persian emperor to help establish the community on a more secure and Jewish basis. In 444 B.C.E., after a good deal of preliminary activity, a great assembly of the people was called at which the Torah was formally read and ratified. This was a signal achievement and, as a result of this event, Ezra has always been regarded as a sort of second Moses who made the Torah the constitution of the new Jewish Commonwealth. Now Ezra, we are told (Ez. 7. 6.), was *Sofer mahir*—a 'ready scribe'. 'That does not signify a copyist with good penmanship, but rather a 'bookish man', a man of the Book, well-versed in the sacred writings, a scholar and student of the Law, the first of a long line of teachers who succeeded him' (Margolis: *Hebrew Scriptures in the Making*); and consequently the reading was done, according to the account in the Book of Nehemiah, distinctly, with the observation of the proper stops, and with accompanying interpretation, with the Levites walking among the people to make sure that they heard and understood what was being read:

> "And they read in the book, in the Law of God, *distinctly*; and they *gave the sense*, and caused them to understand the reading (or, perhaps, 'the text')"—(Neh. 8. 8).[1]

Ezra, had, in fact, begun the task of the commentator and it seems that he had fitted himself carefully for the task of exposition—

> "For Ezra had set his heart to *seek the law* of the Lord, and to do it, and to teach in Israel statutes and ordinances."
> —(Ez. 7. 10.)[2]

The verb used here *darash*, 'to seek', means 'to investigate',—to examine the text, to enquire into what it means; so much so that subsequently the rabbis coined from the same root the noun *Midrash*, denoting the exposition of the Scripture.

Now while the history of formal Biblical interpretation is thus seen to date back to the activity of Ezra the Scribe, it should be understood that, from the point of view of Jewish tradition, the exposition of the text is as old as the text itself. For side by side with the Written Law—*Torah SheBichtav*, according to Jewish tradition, there has always existed, ever since the days of Moses, the Oral Law—*Torah SheB'al Pe*. It would have been impossible to understand and observe the precepts of the former without the interpretation which

3

was at hand in the tradition of the Unwritten Law—which can therefore be regarded as a form of commentary. This applies not only to points of law, but to the narrative portions of the text also—and traces of that tradition ('Biblical Midrash' we might call it) are often found to have been incorporated into later books of the Bible. Let us note a few examples.

Numbers (ch. 20) records Moses' sin in striking the rock when God had told him to speak to it in the presence of the people. Moreover, Moses momentarily displays a lack of faith—

"Shall we bring forth water for you from this rock?"

Some explanation of Moses' action seems called for; and we find one provided in Psalms 106. 33 where we read:—

"For they embittered his spirit, and he spoke rashly with his lips",

i.e., their incessant grumbling embittered him and caused him to lose his self-control so that he uttered rash words.

Again, Jeremiah's prophecy (25. 11–12 and 29. 10) that the Babylonian captivity would last seventy years does not indicate exactly from when and until when; but the Book of Daniel (ch. 9) comments on this prophecy and offers the clue to help us arrive at the conclusion that the termination of the seventy years' exile would be marked by the dedication of the new Temple:—

"and to anoint the most holy place" (9. 24).

For a third illustration, we may compare the account of the consecration of the first Temple by Solomon (I Kings 8) with the corresponding passage in the Book of Chronicles. In the first account we read:

4

"And Solomon held the feast at that time ... seven days and seven days. ... On the eighth day he sent the people away ..." (8. 65–66.)

But the phrase 'seven days and seven days' is ambiguous, nor is it clear whether the 'eighth day' refers to the first or the second 'seven days'. More especially, we want to know what was the relationship between the Feast of Dedication of the Temple and the Feast of Succot, and in what order they were held. These matters are made clear by the reference in II Chronicles (7. 8–10) where we read:

"So Solomon held the feast at that time seven days ... and on the eighth day they held a solemn assembly; for they kept the dedication of the altar seven days, and the Feast (i.e. Succot) seven days. And on the twenty third day of the seventh month he sent the people away to their tents, joyful and glad of heart ..."

In other words, the first 'seven days' were the Feast of Dedication and the second 'seven days' were the Feast of Tabernacles, after which, on the eighth day, a special 'solemn assembly' (*Shemini Atzeret*) was held when the King bade his subjects farewell and gave them leave to depart—which they did thereafter, namely on the twenty third day of the month. Here again, then, we see how one Biblical text serves as a commentary to explain another more obscure one.

The Book of Chronicles contains many similar expositions in which the intention is to clarify earlier writings in the light of the views and traditions currently held and taken for granted. And it was not only textual clarification that concerned the writers; they often provide explanations for what may seem, in the earlier books, to present moral or theological problems—in the same way that, as we noted, the psalmist offers a mitigating circumstance explaining Moses' sin at the Waters of Meriba. Why, for example, should Saul have fallen in battle, and why was he not blessed to establish a dynasty of his own? Chronicles explains it thus:

> "So Saul died for his transgression which he committed against the Lord ... and also for that he asked counsel of a ghost to enquire thereby, and inquired not of the Lord. Therefore He slew him and turned the Kingdom unto David the son of Jesse"—(I Chron. 10. 13–14).

Why should the new young King Solomon have gone to sacrifice and pray at the altar at Gibeon (I Kings 3. 4) rather than to the Ark in Jerusalem? Again the Chronicler is more helpful and explicit: He went to Gibeon—

> "For there was the tent of meeting of God, which Moses the servant of the Lord had made in the wilderness; ... Moreover the brazen altar, that Bezalel ... had made, was there before the Tabernacle of the Lord"—(II Chron. 1. 3, 5).

And, to give one more example, why were the glory and merit of building the Temple to be Solomon's and not his father David's? Solomon's own bald reference to the matter—

> "But the Lord said unto David my father, Whereas it was in thy heart to build a house for My name, thou didst well that it was in thy heart; nevertheless thou shalt not build the house; but thy son ... he shall build the house for My name"—(I Kings 8. 18–19).

was unsatisfying, and again the Chronicler provided the answer to the inevitable questionings:

> "Thou hast shed blood abundantly and hast made great

wars. Thou shalt not build a house unto My name, because thou hast shed much blood ...";

on the other hand, Solomon shall build it because—

"his name will be *Shelomo* and I will give *Shalom* (peace) and quietness unto Israel in his days"—(I Chron. 22. 8–9).

These examples—and their number can be multiplied—give evidence of the vitality of the oral tradition in ancient Bible times. This process of interpreting the written text was eventually to be developed to a very great degree by the rabbis of the Talmud. But the path was shown to them by their predecessors, the Scribes, the first of whom we have been meeting in the Books of Daniel, Ezra and Chronicles.

2

The Scribes and the Targums

THE GREAT problem which faced Ezra upon his arrival in Jerusalem was the danger of assimilation for the newly-established community. During all the period of the Babylonian exile the Samaritans had grown in number and, while they were based on a small nucleus of original Israelites from the north of the country, they were now completely mixed with foreign colonists, not only in blood, but also in cultural standards and mode of spiritual expression. As a consequence, Ezra set himself to prevent mixed marriages between the new settlers of Judea, who had recently returned from Babylon, and their Samaritan neighbours. He also determined to abolish the village shrines which had come to abound everywhere and which were a serious rival to the newly-consecrated Temple in Jerusalem. It may be noted, in passing, that these local temples and altars had been the scenes of often degraded and vile forms of worship since the days of the prophets, whose anger they had constantly provoked. Ezra did not simply denounce these idolatrous trends. He offered a substitute in the form of the *Synagogue* which, as an institution, had already been given some form in the Babylonian exile. In the literature of the time, soon after Ezra, we find the term *Bet Hamidrash*, or House of Exposition, used frequently of the lecture-house which was an essential part of the Synagogue. Unquestionably, the Synagogue once more, as in the Babylonian exile, rallied the people, became their focal centre in every village, and was the saviour of Judaism. When, a century after Ezra, the Persian period ended and the conflict began between Judaism and Hellenism, the Synagogue had become a fundamental institution in the land. Services were held not only on Sabbaths and festivals, but also on the ordinary market-days—Mondays and Thursdays—so that the peasant who came to town on those days could also make his way to the Synagogue, not alone for prayer but also to hear the Torah read and expounded.

Here we see the most important aspect, with the most permanent results, of the work of Ezra the Scribe and his followers. They prevented the community from being overcome by ignorance. They provided the channels for the knowledge of Scripture to reach the common people. Ultimately, it was this very factor which enabled Jewish life to survive the destruction of the Temple, for by that time the Synagogue had been fitted to take its place.

When we talk of the Scribes (*Soferim*) we have in mind that body of teachers which was begun by Ezra and went on for at least two centuries and whose main task was to preserve intact the text of the holy Books and interpret them to the people. Like Ezra himself, they were all 'ready scribes in the Law of Moses'—both in the sense that they were able to write or copy the text of the scrolls and also because they were able to interpret that text. It is more than probable that, especially from the latter point of view, the Scribes are to be identified with the 'Men of the Great Synagogue'[4] of whom we are told in the Mishna (*Avot* 1) that 'they said three things: Be deliberate in Judgment; raise up many disciples; and make a fence round the Torah.' It was the Scribes who established schools and 'raised up many disciples'. In particular, they followed with meticulous care the procedure which had been adopted at Ezra's classic assembly of the people:—"So they read in the Book of the Law of God

9

distinctly, and gave the *sense*, and caused them to understand the reading"—(Neh. 8).

A very early source quoted in the Talmud (*Meg.* 3a) explains the verse to mean that first they read the Hebrew text, then they translated it into the vernacular, taking care to divide the text into recognised sections: *Vayavinu Bamikra* ("And they caused them to understand the text")—this refers, according to one view, to the traditional understanding, or the laws traditionally derived from the given text. That is, whatever laws they taught to the people, they always deduced them directly from a Biblical passage, although sometimes they instituted what we might call by-laws—and what they referred to as 'making a fence round the Torah' in order to safeguard it.

To the Scribes it was clear that the only hope of off-setting Hellenism as a cultural movement lay in a strong Jewish educational programme among the masses; and, with this end in view, they applied themselves in many directions. They laid the foundations for a formalised liturgy to enable the unlearned to take part in worship and they laboured to revive the knowledge and use of the Hebrew language which had been largely forgotten during the Babylonian exile. It was this last factor which made it so vitally important to translate and explain the meaning of the Bible text. At first it was still sufficient to explain difficult words and expressions in simpler, spoken Hebrew—which later developed into the fine literary Hebrew of the Mishna; but the influence of the environment was strong, so that gradually it became necessary to translate passages into the Aramaic vernacular—and it was from these translations that, eventually, there grew the complete Aramaic version of the Bible known popularly, to this day, as the *Targum*.

As a matter of fact, there are, or there were, several Targums. The one that is best known and that is still frequently printed in many editions of the Bible together with the Hebrew original, goes by the name of *Targum Onkelos*. This was already regarded as a sort of official Targum (or Aramaic vernacular version) to the Torah in talmudic times; and in the third century it apparently gained such wide currency and acceptance throughout the Babylonian Schools that it was often referred to also as the 'Babylonian Targum'. But most scholars appear to agree that it originally came to Babylon from Palestine where it took shape mainly in the school of Akiva—i.e. in the second century, soon after the destruction of the Temple. There is indeed a passage in the Talmud (*Meg.* 3a)[5] which discusses the authorship of the Targum and assigns it to Onkelos the Proselyte:

"R. Jeremiah (or, according to another version, R. Hiyya bar Abba) said: The Targum to the Torah (i.e. Pentateuch) was composed by Onkelos the Proselyte at the dictation (or under the instruction) of R. Eliezer and R. Jehoshua."

But it would seem that there was some confusion here, for, in the Jerusalem Talmud, the corresponding passage reads (*Jer. Meg.* 71c):

"*Aquila* the Proselyte translated the Torah in the presence of R. Eliezer and R. Jehoshua, who praised him in the words of the psalmist (45. 3): 'Thou art fairer than the children of men: grace is poured into thy lips; therefore God hath blessed thee for ever'."

Now this Aquila is elsewhere known to us as Aquilas the Proselyte, the author of a Greek translation of Scripture in the early part of the second century, R. Akiva being his teacher in addition to the R. Eliezer and R. Jehoshua mentioned above. Very little was known about this Greek translation, because it was lost, and only in recent times have fragments of the work been recovered among Schechter's finds in the Cairo Geniza, from which it would appear that this was a very literal translation of the text. On the other hand, there are many references in the Talmud to Aquilas himself, his origin and his conversion to Judaism. He is said to have been a nephew of the Roman Emperor Hadrian and to have been attracted to Judaism through his study of the Torah while he was in Palestine. This pious proselyte left his mark in many ways. Apart from his Greek translation, there are many Greek words in the Talmud and Midrashim which are thought to have been introduced by him. Moreover it is almost certain that when the Talmud referred (in *Meg.* 3a) to the tradition of the Targum having been written by Onkelos the Proselyte, they really were mistaking the name for Aquilas the Proselyte and his Greek Targum; whereas the Babylonian Aramaic Targum was of separate origin, having grown up, also in Palestine, on the foundations laid by the Scribes. The mistaken identity is understandable, because there was indeed another proselyte called Onkelos (a nephew of Titus) about whose conversion many anecdotes are recorded in the Babylonian Talmud (e.g. *Gittin* 50a; *Av. Zar.* 11a) and who was well known in Babylon, while hardly anything was known there about the earlier Palestinian Aquilas. Be this as it may, the name of Onkelos remained stuck fast to the Babylonian Targum and its reading was, in later centuries, enjoined almost as a sacred ritual requirement.

The passage in *Meg.* 3a which ascribes the Pentateuchal Targum to Onkelos, goes on to say:

> "Jonathan ben Uzziel composed the Targum to the Prophets from the mouths of Haggai, Zecharia and Malachi."

—the inference being that it was based on old traditions going back to the last prophets. Once again, then, while its formal author is Jonathan b. Uzziel, a pupil of Hillel, this work also must be seen as a product of the activity of the Scribes. Jonathan's action in writing this Targum is depicted as an act of daring novelty; for the talmudic passage goes on to say that the entire land of Israel shook and a heavenly Voice cried out:

> "Who hath revealed My secrets to the children of men? Jonathan b. Uzziel stood up and said: I have revealed them. Be it known to Thee that I did it not for my glory nor for the glory of my father's house, but only for Thy glory, so that there shall not be increasing dissension in Israel. Moreover he wanted to reveal the Targum of the *Ketuvim* (Hagiographa); but a heavenly Voice went forth and said: Enough! For the Messianic end is revealed therein."[6]

Let us now select one or two examples illustrating the method adopted by the Scribes and their pupils in interpreting Scripture. We have already observed that, in the early days, before Hebrew had been displaced by Aramaic as the common spoken language of the man-in-the-street, it had been necessary to translate difficult Hebrew expressions in the text into simpler Hebrew words. Many of these renderings have been preserved in the old Midrashic literature, for example the *Mechilta*. Thus, referring to the Paschal offering (Ex. 12. 9) the verse says, 'Eat it not *Na*', and this is explained: "the word *Na* means nothing other than *Chai*— i.e. raw". "And thus shall ye eat it"—means 'like those setting forth on a journey'.[7] "And it came to pass, when Pharaoh had sent the people away *V'lo Nacham*—God did not lead them by way of the land of the Philistines, etc. ..." (Ex. 13. 17); on which the comment was—"This word *Nacham* means 'guiding' or 'leading'." And the verse: "Thou shalt not be *extortionate* to a stranger, nor *oppress* him", is explained:—'Be not extortionate *in words*, nor oppress him with *money*.'

At the same time, there were other passages in which the Scribes permitted themselves greater freedom and the Targum versions of, say, Jacob's blessing (Gen. 49), the blessing of Moses (Deut. 33), the Song of Deborah (Judges 5) and similarly difficult chapters, are full of homiletical interpretation. And the Scribes permitted themselves the same freedom in rendering passages which offended their sense of due respect either to God or the early heroes of Israel. Perhaps here we have traces of the allegorical method developed by the contemporary Greeks. Thus—"And the Lord went down to see the city" (Gen. 11. 5) is translated: —'The Lord revealed Himself to punish the acts of the city.'[8] And the verse: "Simeon and Levi are brothers; weapons of violence are in their habitations" (Gen. 49. 5) is explained:—

'Mighty men; their habitation is in the land.'[9]

The work of the pious and faithful Scribes opened the way to the development of the whole rich homiletical midrashic literature while preserving intact the original text of Holy Writ. For centuries to come, that literature was to bring comfort and strength to learned and ignorant alike.

3

Fixing the Canon

In CONSIDERING the basic contributions of the Scribes in the field of Bible interpretation, it is important to remember that it was at this time that the Bible itself was being set in the form and order by which we know it today. This 'fixing of the Canon', as the process is called, was the most permanent achievement of the period of the Second Temple; while the finishing touches were not added until the end of the first century C.E., the work was substantially completed by the time of the Maccabees—that is, by the Scribes.

It was the Greeks who used the word *Canon* in relation to the composition of the Bible,—the term itself meaning literally 'a rod', and hence 'norm' or 'law'; and though the Hebrew word *kane* also means 'rod', this term seems not to have been current in Jewish literature. On the other hand, the idea involved in 'canonicity'—i.e. in determining which books should be included in and which excluded from Scripture—was essentially Jewish in origin. In earliest times, the books of the prophets and 'other holy writings' were separate volumes or scrolls. Thus Daniel (9. 2) says:—"I, Daniel, meditated in *the Books*"; and it is from the Greek rendering of this word, *Biblia*, that we get the English *Bible*. It is clear, then, that we are speaking not of one book or volume, but rather of a whole collection—a library—of books. So far as most of them were concerned—the Torah or five books of Moses, for example, and the books of the Prophets—there was never any doubt about their sacred and inspired character. It was only after the return from Babylonian exile, when, as time went on, more books were added, that discussion arose as to whether these later works were to be thought of in the same way and accorded the same reverence. It was then that the process of selection began.

According to a classic passage in the Talmud (*Bava Batra* 14b–15a) the collection of Scriptural books was already known and accepted in the days of Ezra. This account gives the order of 'the Books' and clearly distinguishes between the *prophets* and the *Ketuvim*, mentioning under the latter heading the books of Ruth, Psalms, Job, Proverbs, Kohelet, Song of Songs, Lamentations, Daniel, Esther, Ezra and Chronicles. The account goes on to give the names of the authors of each work, concluding as follows: "The Men of the Great Synagogue wrote Ezekiel, the Twelve (Prophets), Daniel and Esther. Ezra wrote his own book and the genealogies of the Book of Chronicles." Now Ezra himself belonged to the 'Men of the Great Synagogue'; consequently, from the fact that he and his work are singled out for special and separate mention at the end of the list, it seems that the assumption was that the Scriptures were actually completed in his time. This was certainly taken for granted in the Greek period. For instance, the writings of the sage Ben Sira (in the third century B.C.E.) show that he was familiar with the Torah and the Prophets in their present form, complete; while the translator of Ben Sira from Hebrew into Greek (about 130 B.C.E.) specifically refers to the Torah, Prophets and 'other writings'. This was, of course, soon after the Maccabean War; and, about the same time, the Book of Maccabees, referring to Nehemiah's work, says (2 *Macc.* 6):

"... how he, founding a library, gathered together the

books about the Kings and Prophets, and the writings of David."

The existence is here assumed of a three-fold division of the sacred books into Torah, Prophets and 'Writings' (*Ketuvim* or Hagiographa) in the time of Nehemiah. The passage in Maccabees goes on to say: "And in like manner also Judas gathered together all those books that had been scattered by reason of the war, and they are with us now."

It is perfectly understandable that during the religious persecution that led to the Maccabean uprising—when scrolls of the Torah were torn and burnt and the study of the sacred literature was punishable by death—these holy books were secreted away and kept in hiding until after the Maccabean War was brought to a successful conclusion. Only then was it possible to bring all these scrolls out of their hiding places; and the reference we have here from the Book of Maccabees shows that the official collection of Scripture was already in being at that time and had long been taken for granted. It was only in connection with the third division, the *Ketuvim*—or 'other writings'—that discussion was to rage during the following two centuries in order to determine which books were to be included as being officially recognised.

The Mishna has a classic passage (*Yad.* ch. 3) in which it discusses the validity of certain books. As a general principle it says:—"All holy writings defile the hands." This expression is the Mishnaic way of defining whether a book should be included in the Canon or not. On the surface, it appears to be an odd expression; but it is in keeping with the general idea that *holy* things were to be set apart from *ordinary* things, and that one had therefore to cleanse oneself both before and after touching a holy thing. There was to be no direct contact between the holy and the ordinary. Hence the rabbis speak of the holy books as 'defiling the hands', meaning thereby that after touching them one should wash one's hands, just as the High Priest had to bathe both before and after performing his sacrifice. In the same way, the priests transferred to their special priestly food (*Teruma*—or heave-offering) the ablutions which were required for the actual sacrifice; and they thus became accustomed to wash their hands both before their meals and after them. Just as the priest was required to wash away, as it were, the holiness of the sacrificial food before proceeding to ordinary mundane affairs, so was it now also enjoined to wash the hands after touching a sacred book. The Mishna (*Yad* 4. 6) records a controversy on this matter between the Pharisees and the Sadducees:—

"The Sadducees said, We complain of you Pharisees for you say that the holy writings defile the hands, while the works of Homer (or, according to one explanation, the heretics) do not defile the hands."[10]

Rabbi Yochanan ben Zakkai replied:

"the holy writings are declared impure because of our reverence for them (i.e. in order to keep them apart), while the heretical books, which we do not revere, are not impure and do not defile the hands."[11]

There was apparently a whole class of books that were looked upon as being beyond the pale. In general, there was an inherent conservatism about adding to the traditional literature, for it was held that divine inspiration as revealed in the Prophets had ceased after Malachi: "After the death of Haggai, Zecharia and Malachi, the Holy Spirit departed from Israel"—(*Sota* 48b).[12] The teaching of Kohelet (*Eccles.* 12.12) was also very much borne in mind: "And further, my son, be admonished by this;" (*Mehema*—lit 'by these') "of making many books there is no end; and much study is a weariness of the flesh." The Midrash makes a play on the word *mehema* (by these), reading it as if it were *mehumma*—'confusion'; and therefore interprets the verse to mean that he who brings more than twenty four books (i.e. the twenty four Books of the Bible) into his house brings confusion. Consequently, goes on the Midrash, the books of Ben Sira may be read but not to the degree of 'weariness of the flesh' (*Eccles. Rabba*). Another Midrash (*Num. Rabba* 14) says: "Twenty four books have I written for you; take heed to add none thereto. Wherefore? Because 'of making many books there is no end'. He who reads one verse not written in the twenty four books is as though he had read in the *Sefarim Hachitzoniim*—the *outside books*; he will find no salvation there."

Thus there were some books which it was, apparently, thought dangerous to read, and among these were the books of the apocrypha which were of late authorship and whose contents and spirit were recognised as moving away from 'official' Judaism. These books were therefore excluded, and were called 'Outside Books'. The Mishna (*Sanh.* 10) went so far as to impose a heavy sanction against the reading of these excluded books, saying, in the name of R. Akiva, that he who reads them 'has no place in the world to come'. The normal method of relegating a book to the 'outside' was by making sure that it was not available for public reading. These books were therefore not kept in the Synagogue, but were hidden away in a separate store-room. The expression describing this action was *bikshu lignoz*—'the authorities sought to store away (hide, secrete) a certain book.' From this word *genoz* we have the now famous term *Geniza* which means, simply, 'store-room'. Storing away a particular book, and thus withdrawing it from public reading, made it 'apocryphal'; whereas, on the other hand, keeping it before the public eye, always available for reading and study, made it 'canonical'.

The struggle that was taking place in the century or so preceding the Christian era between the Pharisees and the Sadducees, together with the dangerous political storms that were gathering over Judea, and the consequent anxiety for Jewish survival, had a great impact on the fixing of the final Canon. In the last days of the Second Temple the Pharisees were in the ascendancy and their separatist tendencies were strengthened by the struggle with Rome, as well as by the growth of the new Christian sect. Pharisaism itself, moreover, had broken away from the former Hasmonean dynasty which, in its latter days, had fraternized too closely with the Sadducees and the ruling foreign powers. The Pharisees had feared that that way lay assimilation. Understandably, therefore, they tended to exclude from the Books of Scripture anything written from the time of the Maccabees onwards; and so even the Book of Maccabees, which is our source for so much of the history of the time, has no place in our Bible.

Whilst discussing the fate of these external books, consideration was also given to the possible exclusion of some books which appear to have been previously accepted. For example, we find serious discussion concerning the *Song of Songs* and *Kohelet* in the Mishna (*Yad.* 3) where, after several views have been stated, we are told:

"R. Shimon b. Azai stated: I have heard a tradition from the seventy two elders on the day that they made R. Eleazar b. Azaria head of the college, that the Song of Songs and Ecclesiastes both defile the hands. R. Akiva said: God forbid! No man in Israel ever disputed about the Song of Songs ... for all the world is not worth the day on which the Song of Songs was given to Israel; for all the Writings are holy, but the Song of Songs is the Holy of Holies. And if anything was in dispute, it could only have been Ecclesiastes."[13]

The reference to R. Eleazar's appointment as head of the College has to do with a most serious and important occasion on which, at a special session at Yavne, in the year 90 C.E., R. Gamliel was deposed and the youthful Eleazar ben Azaria was elected in his place. At that same session, a resolution was passed excluding the 'sectarian tracts and books of the heretics', Ben Sira, and all books written from then on (vide *Tosefta Yadayim*). This appears to have been the final act—and, incidentally, probably the only formal act—by which the Scriptures as we know them were defined. In actual fact the Canon had been an accepted entity for at least two hundred and fifty years —an inheritance from the days of the 'Men of the Great Synagogue'. With the destruction of the Second Temple at the hands of Rome and the dangers inherent in the new situation, the Pharisees formally closed the Bible by ensuring the permanent exclusion of those writings which failed to come up to their standards.

The work of the Scribes was done. The Scriptures which they had brought back from the Babylonian captivity had been made safe against the storms and winds which were again to rage over the Jewish people.

4

The Mishna

THE PROCESS of interpreting Scripture, for which the foundations were laid, as we have seen, by the Scribes, was continued by their successors whom we call *Tannaim*. The word *Tanna* is Aramaic, and is the equivalent of the Hebrew root *Shanah* which means 'to repeat'—and hence 'to teach by repetition'. When we bear in mind the fact that, in those ancient days, whatever was learnt had to be retained in the memory (and not in written form), the importance of continuous repetition as a means of teaching is clear. The *Tannaim* therefore were teachers who transmitted the tradition by word of mouth and by means of repetition; and the substance of what they taught was called, from the Hebrew root, *Mishna*.

Now the Scribes had been chiefly concerned with explaining the text of the Written Torah; and their expositions, which often involved searching into veiled meanings of words or expressions, or oral traditions, or homiletical and allegorical moralising, gradually built up the *Midrash*—that is a body of interpretation based on the deducing of ideas and teachings directly from the Scriptural verse. The *Tannaim* who inherited this collection of Midrashim in about the first century B.C.E., greatly expanded it; and so voluminous did it become that the Sages began to distinguish between those Midrashim which were concerned with the legal portions of the Torah, and which they called *Midrash Halacha*, and those which dealt with the Biblical narratives, and which they called *Midrash Aggada*. This

22

whole Midrashic literature arose entirely from the Scriptural text, to which it usually served as a sort of systematic verse by verse running commentary; and it was this which chiefly distinguished it from the *Mishna* which taught *Halachot* —rules, laws—independently of their Scriptural basis. The essential and characteristic element in the Mishna is its acceptance and setting down of the traditions of the elders, sometimes spoken of simply as *Kabbala*—"accepted ancient tradition"—and at other times as *Halacha L'Moshe MiSinai*— "The Law as given to Moses on Sinai". For the hypothesis was that here was the Oral Law—*Torah SheB'Al Pe*— which was taught from Mount Sinai at the same time as the Written Law and which claimed the same divine origin and consequently the same authority and binding force. Indeed the Mishna itself asserts (*Sanh.* 11. 3).

"Greater stringency applies to the observance of the words of the Scribes (i.e. oral tradition) than to the observance of the words of the Written Torah;"

and this seemingly bold assertion implies that the Oral Law, on the one hand claims the same authority and continuity as the Written Law, and on the other hand serves as its living interpretation and essential complement.

At the same time, in spite of the independence of the *Mikra*—the Written Biblical text—the Mishna contains a number of instances of the midrashic method, testifying to the strength of the latter's popularity. *Sanh.* 2. 4–5, for instance, is a typical example of a Midrash—a verse by verse commentary—on Deut. 17. 15–19 giving the laws regulating the position of the King:—

" 'Nor shall he multiply wives unto himself'—eighteen only. R. Judah says: He may multiply them to himself provided they do not turn away his heart. R. Simeon

says: If there was but *one* and she would turn away his
heart, he may not marry her. Why then is it written, 'Nor
shall he multiply wives unto himself?'—Even though
they be like Abigail. 'He shall not multiply horses unto
himself'—enough for his chariot only. 'Neither shall he
multiply to himself silver and gold'—enough to supply
his soldiers' wants only. He must write out a scroll of the
Torah for himself; when he goes forth to battle he shall
take it forth with him, and when he returns he shall bring
it back with him. When he sits in judgment it shall be
with him, and when he sits at meat it shall be before him;
for it is written: 'It shall be with him and he shall read
therein all the days of his life.' "

A similar style is found also in *Mishna Sota*, ch. 8, in its
interpretation of the Deuteronomy passage describing the
priest's exhortation to the people on the eve of battle
(Deut. 20); and again the ninth chapter of *Sota* with its
almost word-for-word explanation of the ritual to be
followed in the event of a person being found murdered
(Deut. 21). These passages are not typical of the style of the
Mishna, which usually makes its point and sets out its law
or its doctrine, without reference to a Biblical source at all.
Thus the very first Mishna reads:

"From what time in the evening may the *Shema* be
recited? From the time when the priests enter the Temple
to eat of their heave-offering until the end of the first
watch. So says R. Eliezer. But the Sages say, Until mid-
night. Rabban Gamliel says, Until the rise of dawn ..."
(*Ber.* 1, 1).

Later talmudical discussion on this passage raised a number
of pertinent questions, such as: What is the Biblical basis
for the Mishna-teacher to assume that the *Shema* has to be

read at all? Moreover, if we are to discuss the times for the reciting of the *Shema*, why begin with the evening? Would it not be more natural to start with the morning duty?— To these and other questions the later Sages of the *Gemara* found answers and support from Biblical verses. But the Mishna is content simply to state the Law, giving the names of the Sages who held differing views and traditions, but not deeming it necessary to state their Biblical authority.

The Mishna itself gives its own account of the origin and history of the Oral Law of which it was the culminating point. A classic passage is the opening chapter of the tractate *Avot* which runs:

> "Moses received the Torah from Sinai and transmitted it to Joshua, and Joshua to the Elders, and the Elders to the Prophets; and the Prophets committed it to the Men of the Great Synagogue."

This brings the tradition down to beyond the time of Ezra. The same passage goes on to state that Simon the Righteous was "of the remnants of the Men of the Great Synagogue" —i.e. he lived perhaps about 200 B.C.E. The line of tradition is then traced through Simon's pupil, Antigonus of Socho, and on through five 'pairs' of Sages (still of the period of the Scribes) to Shemaia and Abtalyon, and to their famous pupil, Hillel, and the latter's equally famous controversial contemporary, Shammai. Thus the chain is brought down to the first century of the current era.

By this time, the Oral Law had grown into a formidable corpus of laws, traditions, precedents and sanctified usages. Inevitably, while the people lived on the basis of a Torah-constitution, the application of the law to daily life, to temple-worship, to trade and domestic relations, as well as in the administration of justice, gave rise to an enormous number of rules and accepted usages invested with sanctity and authority. Moreover, the people had passed through a number of great social upheavals in the course of several centuries. The Babylonian exile, the Return and the Building of the Second Temple, the impact of Greek civilisation, and now the rise of the new Christian ideas—all had presented a challenge and necessitated adjustment in the religious authority and law no less than in the social and economic sense. Account must also be taken of the difficulty of transmitting this vast mass of religious and legal precept, especially as it was unthinkable to those early Sages that it should be committed to writing. Even as late as the third century, the Sage Jochanan ben Nappacha said:

> "Whosoever writes out the *Halacha* is as one who burns up the Torah"(*Tem.* 14b).

And it was about the time of Hillel that an attempt began to be made to introduce some order into the voluminous material, so that it should be the more easily memorised.

Born in Babylon, Hillel came to Palestine to study under Shemaia and Abtalyon, and in the reign of Herod he was appointed *Nasi* or President of the Sanhedrin. He was particularly famed for his gentle and peace-loving character, and his proverbial patience has become classically associated with his reply to the heathen who asked to be taught the Torah 'while he stood on one foot'. "Do not unto thy neighbour what is hateful to thyself"—replied Hillel undaunted; "the rest is commentary; go and learn." It was this Hillel who laid the foundations for the work of classifying the Oral Law into what eventually grew to be the Mishna. Among Hillel's pupils was Rabbi Jochanan ben Zakkai who witnessed the destruction of the Second Temple and the Jewish Commonwealth by the Romans in 70 c.e. At this time of indescribable horror, when it seemed to many that Judaism and the Jewish people had met their doom,

Jochanan ben Zakkai rallied the remnants of the people and established a new centre at Yavne. 'The Vineyard of Yavne', it was called; and it was from here that the Sage embarked upon a programme of spiritual reconstruction. Yavne soon became authoritative; the Supreme Court and Sanhedrin were established there, and the process of introducing order and system into the teaching of the Oral Law went forward. For sixty years (70–130 C.E.) there ensued a fruitful period of peace—broken by the wave of intense religious persecution which swept Palestine after the accession of Hadrian as the new Roman Emperor. A heroic but hopeless revolt—the last bid for Jewish independence from the Roman yoke—was led by Bar Kochba, and, with the ruthless crushing of this struggle, the Sage Rabbi Akiva died a martyr's death. Akiva was by far the most outstanding figure of his time and seems to have made the greatest contribution in the development of the Mishna. He must have had an amazing power of memory and is referred to in the Talmud (*Git.* 67a) as "A swollen treasury", —which expression Rashi explains (*ad. loc.*) by quoting another old talmudic source (*Avot de'R. Natan*). "To what might Rabbi Akiva be likened?"—runs this note. "To a labourer who took up his basket and went out to the field. When he found wheat, he cut some and put it in the basket. When he found barley he put that in; and so also with lentils and spelt. When he returned home, he sorted them out one from the other. So is it with R. Akiva. When he studied with his masters, he learnt Bible, Halacha, Midrash and Agada. He mastered them all and then arranged the various subjects in rings, classifying them and separating one from the other."

Based on Akiva's work, his disciples, chief among whom must be mentioned R. Meir (*c.* 160), prepared collections of Mishnayot for their own use. This led to the existence of a number of variant versions—with consequent confusion. It was R. Yehuda Hanasi (*c.* 200) who finally assembled and collated all those collections and produced a standard edition of The Mishna which has remained authoritative to this day. There is no doubt, however, that the principal source used by R. Yehuda was the basic collection compiled by Akiva. The Mishna itself refers to this in a number of places. For example *Sanh.* 3. 4 states:

> "Such was the Mishna of R. Akiva. But the First Mishna taught ..."[14]

This seems to point to a collection (the "First Mishna") even earlier than Akiva's. In other passages, we find the statement:

> "Such was the First Mishna; but the later Bet Din ruled ..."—(*Git.* 5. 6; *Ket.* 5. 3).[15]

The importance of R. Akiva's contribution can be seen from yet another statement by Jochanan ben Nappacha who was a young contemporary of R. Yehuda Hanasi. He states (*Sanh.* 86a):[16]

> "Anonymous rulings in the Mishna are those of R. Meir. ... And all are according to the teachings of R. Akiva."

It was fitting that this great work should have been completed by R. Judah the Prince (or, as he was also called, *Hakadosh*, 'the holy one') who not only was the greatest Sage of his time but also traced his illustrious descent from Hillel, who had laid the foundations for the Mishna. There were inevitably many traditional 'mishnayot' which were omitted from the final compilation as part of the general sifting of the material. These became known by the term

Baraita—'external mishna',—and they were remembered and often referred to by subsequent teachers. For many centuries to come, both in Babylon and in Palestine, Rabbi Judah's Mishna was the basis for all religious, legal and literary activity.

5

Rules of Exposition

WE HAVE now sketched the growth of Biblical exposition through the Babylonian exile, the work of Ezra and the Scribes, and the Codification of the Oral Law in the form of the Mishna. In this long period of about seven hundred years, from Ezra until Rabbi Judah's compilation of the Mishna at the beginning of the third century, there had been not only many contributors but also various approaches so far as method was concerned. We have seen how, stemming from Ezra himself, there had developed the style of interpretation known as *Derash*—i.e. searching into the meaning of the text from a subjective point of view. In short, the intention here was chiefly to find some authority in a Biblical verse for currently held concepts and ideas, traditions and teachings, so as to give them validity. It was, of course, generally believed that the words of Scripture could have many meanings and this enabled the teachers to find in them homilies for the religious edification and moral instruction of their times. Gradually, these explanations came to be divided into the Midrashim of the Halacha (i.e. to do with legal matters) and the Midrashim of Aggada—dealing with the non-legal portions of Scripture; and finally there was the whole corpus of law in the form of memorized tradition transmitted from generation to generation, until it was put together in the *Mishna*. In all this period, the Sages were not only given over to the task of collecting and arranging the teachings that were already in their possession, but were also constantly grappling with their own re-statement and

30

re-interpretation of the Law in the light of the needs of their own times.

We have seen how the Midrashim were explanations of the Scriptural text based on a careful adherence to the text itself and commenting on it verse by verse—or sometimes even word by word. But this was only one of the approaches to the problem of interpreting the Scriptures. Altogether, we find that there were four early methods that formed the basis for the teachings in the schools of the different masters. They are usually referred to by the mnemonic PARDES, i.e. *Peshat, Remez, Derash, Sod*; the word *Pardes*, meaning 'orchard', is found, in this connection, used allegorically in a well-known passage in the Talmud (*Hag.* 14b):[17]

> "Four Sages entered Paradise" (lit. "the Orchard") "Ben Azai, Ben Zoma, Acher and R. Akiva ... Ben Azai looked and died ...; Ben Zoma went mad ...; Acher destroyed the plants; and only R. Akiva came out unhurt" (lit. "in peace").

The passage is of special interest because of the light it throws on the theological speculations of the greatest Jewish minds at the dawn of the Christian era. The one referred to as *Acher* is a story in himself. His real name was Elisha ben Abuya. At some stage in his career, he became an apostate and from that time on his colleagues would not even refer to him by his real name, but only in terms normally used to designate an object of contempt. "Acher" means "another thing". Many anecdotes are related of this Acher. He is reputed to have been an informer during the Hadrianic persecutions and to have lured young pupils away from their Torah studies. This is indeed a possible meaning of the words "Acher destroyed the plants"—that is, he in effect 'killed' the pupils by taking them away from the Torah. The reason given in the Talmud for Elisha's apostasy is that he saw how a man had lost his life in trying to fulfil a commandment for which the Torah had promised the reward of long life. This, it is said, destroyed his faith. (*Hullin* 142a, end.)

There must have been a good deal of eagerness to make contact with the intellectual influence of the non-Jewish world of those days, and this no doubt encouraged the delving into the realms of mysticism. This is all symbolised by the term *Pardes* ('Orchard') from which only Akiva was strong enough to emerge unharmed. Eventually, this word *Pardes* came to be used to denote the various methods of uncovering the meaning of Scripture. *Peshat* is the term used to denote the primary sense of the text, the plain meaning that is brought out at first reading. In contrast with the *Derash*, the *Peshat* gives the simple, natural explanation of the literal sense.

The third approach to the text is that called *Remez*— 'hint' or 'allusion'. This method is based on the assumption that the words of Scripture are not necessarily to be taken at their face meaning, but are meant to convey a hint of something completely different. The words of the text are seen as a kind of sign or symbol stirring up in our thoughts ideas that are only hinted at in the text. An example of this method of interpretation is the well-known comment on the passage in Exodus describing the war with Amalek when Moses was told to hold his hands aloft:

> "Did then the hands of Moses make the war or break the war?" asks the Commentary. "No! But Scripture here tells us that as long as Israel looked towards heaven and subjected their hearts to their Father in Heaven, they were victorious, but if they failed to do so they were defeated."

The same explanation is given for the brazen serpent (Num. 21) which was supposed to heal the people who looked up at it. It was the implied lesson that they were to look upwards towards their Father in Heaven that brought healing. (Mishna R.H. 3. 8.) Similarly, there are a number of other religious matters commanded in Scripture—such as Tephillin (phylacteries), Tzitzit (fringes), Mezuza, and the Sabbath itself—which were intended as a symbol (*Remez*) or outward reminder of the lesson of faith contained in them. This form of interpretation does indeed take account of the primary meaning of the text (*Peshat*), but it also assumes that this very *Peshat* itself is intended to lead us to another oblique, and perhaps higher, meaning.

As against this, there is yet the fourth attitude to the understanding of Scripture, which boldly asserts that the *Peshat* is to be wholly discarded; in other words, that the text says one thing and means another. This is known as the allegorical method, referred to in Hebrew by the word *Sod* meaning "secret". According to this type of interpretation, for instance, the Genesis story of the Garden of Eden is not to be understood literally as if there really was a garden and a tree and a serpent and Adam and Eve; but all these are to be read as symbols representing something else;—the Tree of Knowledge is a figure for Intellect; the serpent stands for Lust; Eve represents emotion or passion, while Adam symbolises the power of thought. This approach to Scripture found a very wide acceptance among the Alexandrine community and it is the most characteristic feature of the work of Philo. But in this approach, the dangers arising from the possibilities of tampering with the true meaning of Scripture are obvious, and consequently it was never very popular in the main Jewish centres. At the same time, something of the sort was certainly known and used in the days of the earliest Scribes. Only this can explain the fact that the Song of Songs—on the face of it a secular love-song—was admitted to the Canon of the Bible. The Scribes were of the opinion that the outer form of this Song was merely a garb covering some deep and hidden meaning of great worth—in fact, that it really spoke of the ideal love between God and the Community of Israel.

Without question, the most fruitful of all the fields of interpretation until the close of talmudic times was the field of Midrash. Whole schools of Midrashim grew up and Rules (*midot*) for the exposition of the Biblical text were drawn up by a number of important Sages. Hillel was the first who compiled a list of seven Rules, though the possibility is that he may have learned them from his teachers, Shemaia and Abtalyon, who were famed as *Darshanim Gedolim*—"Great midrashic teachers." (*Pes.* 70b.) Subsequently, these seven Rules were expanded by R. Ishmael to thirteen, and still more were added, until the number grew to thirty two in the time of R. Eliezer ben Jose of Galilee. These Rules were developed to such an extent that their employment sometimes seemed artificial. Rabbi Nechunya ben Hakane is reported (*Shev.* 26a) to have interpreted the whole Torah by the Rule of *K'lal u-Prat*—i.e. a general statement followed by details already understood in the general proposition (in which case the general proposition is limited to the things specified).

It was the great Rabbi Akiva of the second century who carried this method to its farthest extreme. He stoutly maintained the view that nothing in the text, not even what seemed to be most insignificant, was without its special meaning. Everything must therefore be interpreted—every seemingly superfluous or redundant word or even letter, every repetition, everything in the text, was sacred and had its purpose. In opposition to this view, Rabbi Ishmael, a great contemporary of Akiva's, maintained that—*Dibra Torah B'LeShon B'nei Adam*—"The Torah speaks in the language of men,"—i.e. it uses the forms and figures and other devices of ordinary human speech, and therefore no special legal deductions may be made from them. Characteristic of the difference between Akiva and Ishmael is the fact, for instance, that Akiva deduced from the one letter *Vav* ('And') that a priest's married daughter who committed adultery should be put to death by fire. To this, R. Ishmael retorted: "Merely because you make this deduction from this one letter, shall we burn the poor woman?" (*Sanh.* 51b).[18]

On another occasion, R. Ishmael said accusingly to another upholder of Akiva's excessively midrashic view: "You say to Scripture—Be silent while I am expounding!" (*Sifra* on Lev. 13. 47)[19]—that is, you don't allow Scripture itself to say what it wants to say!

The disciples of Ishmael held their own and it was from this school, called De Be Rabbi Ishmael, that the first midrashic commentaries to the Torah went forth, viz. the *Mechilta* to the Book of Exodus, and the *Sifre* to Numbers and Deuteronomy. It was due to their influence also that later Babylonian teachers, *Amoraim*, laid down the principle: *En Mikra Yotze Midde Peshuto*—"Nothing can over-ride the primary straightforward meaning (*Peshat*) of the text"— (*Shab.* 63a).

6

The Massora

THE EXPANSION of Christian influence in Palestine was accompanied by a gradual thinning out of the Jewish population. Modern archaeological research has brought to light an impressive series of once magnificent synagogues, particularly in Galilee. Even now, excavations are proceeding at the site of Bet Shearim, where the houses and palaces must have been truly fine buildings. But Jewish life in the Holy Land was very much on the decline. For a period, the Romans enjoined tolerance; but later this policy was changed in the hope that the Jews might be converted to the new faith under pressure. Many discriminatory laws were introduced, and in 425 C.E. the Patriarchate was entirely abolished and its emoluments diverted to the treasury of the Emperor. Thus the last vestige of Jewish independence was swept away. Jewish autonomy, which had existed since the return from Exile nearly a thousand years earlier, was brought to an end, and the headship and control of Jewish affairs in Palestine passed into the hands of the Romans. A century or so later, the Code of Justinian I even tried to influence the internal affairs of the Synagogue, by stipulating the reading of a Greek translation of the Scriptures.

However, the Arab conquest of the land in the seventh century brought relief. One of the later teachers, the Gaon Yehudai (Gaon of Sura Academy, mid-eighth century) acknowledged the fact in the words: "When the Ishmaelites came they left us free to occupy ourselves with the Torah." Though, at first, no Jews were supposed to reside in the

36

Holy City, it was not long before a Jewish community sprang up there. The Galilean schools, especially, were re-organized, and Tiberias became again a centre of scholastic activity. The advent of Islam meant not only the freeing of the Jewish Community from the yoke of physical persecution. Even of greater moment, perhaps, was its influence on the cultural and spiritual life of Jewry for the next few centuries. In particular, the enthusiasm of the Arabs for the Koran constituted a challenge to the Jews and stimulated them further to protect their own Scriptures and to defend their traditional text. The whole world of Islamic thought which now opened before them led to the need for further interpretation and presentation of the Jewish religious position, and the work of most of the Jewish philosopher-commentators of this period was prompted by these considerations. But, first and foremost, the need was felt for establishing the text of the Jewish Scriptures on a firm basis so that the traditional text and understanding should not be lost in an uncertain and changing world.

Those who undertook this task became known as the Massoretes,—those who established the *Massora* (tradition). *Massoret Seyag La Torah*—"The Massora (tradition) is a fence to the Torah", says the Mishna (*Avot* 3. 13). For many centuries, this had been accepted and unchallenged. The text of Scripture was read and understood according to the meaning and rendering handed down from generation to generation. From earliest times, it had been recognised that errors might creep into the text. The Scroll of the Torah contained no vowels or accents, and so they have come down to us to this day. In the process of their being copied, they were inevitably subject to the fate of all human work, —i.e. to mistakes creeping in. To meet this difficulty, one correct authorised copy was always kept in a safe place; and the meticulous care with which the scrolls were scrutinized is illustrated by a recorded statement (*Soferim* 6. 4) which runs: "Rabbi Shimon ben Lakish said, Three copies of the Torah were found in the hall of the Temple. They were named the *Me'ona* Scroll, the *Zatute* Scroll, and the *Hee* Scroll. In the first the word *Ma'on* was written instead of *Meona* (Deut. 33. 27). In the second the word *Na'are* (Exod. 24. 5) was written *Zatute*, and in the third the word *Hu* is written as *Hee* eleven times. The reading that was found only in one of the copies was rejected and the reading of the other two was accepted. The accepted text has therefore *Meona, Na'are* and *Hee*."

Here we have an example of early massoretic work in transcribing and multiplying copies of the Torah. Sometimes, it was necessary to draw special attention to some parts of the text—because the meaning was obscure, or because an old traditional homiletic interpretation was associated with the word or words, or perhaps to guard against certain letters or words being later thought superfluous and hence being erased. Now the text itself was fixed and was not permitted to be altered in any way, and therefore the Massoretes adopted other expedients in order to make sure that the traditional *understanding* of the text—the *Mikra*, the way it was to be *read*—should not be forgotten. Confronted by a similar situation nowadays, we should resort to a lengthy series of footnotes and marginal notes; but these were forbidden to be entered in the holy scrolls, and instead only some mnemonic devices were used so as to call to mind the point associated with the particular passage. Thus, some words have dots over their letters, and, in later times, commentators have offered various possible explanations of their original purpose and meaning. For instance, in the Genesis account of the meeting of Jacob with Esau (33. 4), we are told how Esau "ran to meet him and embraced him, and he fell on his neck *Vayishakehu*—and he kissed him". The word *Vayishakehu* has dots over each letter and two traditional explanations are reported. One holds that the dots are to indicate that the kiss was false and insincere, while the other (attributed to R. Shimon bar Yochai) says: "One would ordinarily have assumed that to be the case because of Esau's known hatred for Jacob; therefore the dots have been placed there to indicate that at that moment Esau's heart was filled with pity and compassion and he *did* kiss Jacob with all his heart"—(*v. Rashi, ad loc.*).[20]

Similarly, we find a few instances where a letter is written *Teluya*—suspended above the line. In the Book of Judges (18. 30) we read how the tribe of Dan "set up for themselves the graven image; and Jonathan the son of Gershom, the son of Manasseh, were priests to the tribes of the Danites until the day of the captivity of the land." Now the letter *Nun* in the word Manasseh is suspended—to indicate that really this Jonathan was the grandson of Moses, but the latter's name was written as Manasseh out of respect and reverence for Moses, so as not to link such a shameful act so blatantly with him.[21]

Already in ancient times there were some words in the text that were deliberately read differently from the way they were written. These substitutions were well known and traditionally handed down by word of mouth; but again, of course, they were not permitted to be written in the scrolls, even as a marginal note. It was only in talmudic times that such marginal notes began to creep into private copies. There were various reasons for these variants. Sometimes it was to prevent a blasphemous thought,— for example, 'to curse God' would be read as 'to bless God'; again, an unseemly word would be replaced by a seemly one; and yet another whole class of these variant-readings were intended to call attention to some homiletic (*midrashic*) meaning to be understood as embodied in the text. In all of these cases, a special terminology came to be used—the Keri and Ketiv—*Keri* is the way the word is to be *read*; the *Ketiv* is the way it is *written*.

While the text of the Scriptures was fixed very early—perhaps two centuries or more B.C.E.—its true preservation and understanding depended for many centuries to come on tradition. Even in the days of the Temple, the standard copy deposited there was only of direct benefit to those who lived near enough to Jerusalem to be able to refer to it. But the large communities everywhere else, and especially in Babylon, were forced to rely on memory and tradition as these were carried mainly by the scholars passing from one community to another. In the course of time, differences began to appear between the versions in Palestine and Babylon, but it is interesting to note that in these matters the Babylonian scholars always deferred to their Palestinian colleagues. "They are experts; we are not," they said. Many were troubled by the danger of the tradition (the *Massora*) being forgotten. The community in Palestine had been severely reduced, both in numbers and learning, by the Romans and Byzantines; and in Babylon, too, the great Schools were closed for most of the sixth century because of persecution. The Sages began, therefore, to devote themselves increasingly to the collection of all the massoretic traditional material and to fixing the text of Scripture permanently on the basis of this material. They became grammarians and applied the rules of the Hebrew language; they fixed the punctuation; they noted every *Keri* and *Ketiv* and all other exceptional readings as handed down by the Massora. But their greatest and most far-reaching legacy was the invention of a whole system of vocalization, of vowel-signs which henceforth made the correct reading and understanding of the text of the Bible available to every man-in-the-street. Apart from fixing the pronunciation of the words, they also added a system of strokes, dots and other signs, known as *Ta'amim*, which determined the grouping of the words in phrases and verses according to the traditional sense, and thus made possible the reading, and even the singing, of the text with proper meaning.

The work of these massoretic (mainly anonymous) teachers went on mainly from the seventh to the tenth centuries, and reached its climax in Tiberias under the authority of Aaron the son of Moshe Ben Asher. He practically brought the Massora to its close by writing a standard Codex of the Bible which was accepted by the entire West, to which, by this time, the centre of Jewish life and influence was moving. During the eleventh, twelfth and thirteenth centuries, the commentators paid great attention to the massoretic notes and tried hard to add their interpretations. But the Massora itself may be said, without exaggeration, to constitute the most important commentary we have to the Bible text, for without those massoretic notes, points and punctuation, we should hardly be able to read that text today.

7

Sa'adya Gaon

THE NEW RELIGION, Islam, which swept across Asia and Africa from the seventh century onwards, released new energies for the study of a number of subjects, like mathematics, astronomy, philosophy and poetry, in which the Jews were drawn to participate. Until now, particularly in Palestine and Babylon, almost the entire preoccupation of the Jewish sages and scholars had been with the Talmud; but now the great outburst of intellectual power which had produced the two Talmuds, and an abundance of other rabbinic literature, had spent its force. Many were now attracted by the new horizons that beckoned and began to doubt the truth of their Jewish traditional beliefs in the face of the new instruments of philosophy and logic; while some even embraced the faith of Islam.

This external challenge was matched, at the same time, by perhaps an even more insidious danger within the Jewish people itself. For the schismatic sect of the Karaites arose in the second half of the eighth century, attacking traditional rabbinic Judaism and aiming at establishing Jewish life and teaching only on the written Scriptures themselves. For a while, it seemed that the traditional leadership of the people was weak and powerless to defend its heritage against this two-fold challenge. But at the end of the ninth century, in this dark time for Judaism, a great champion and defender of the rabbinic position arose in the person of Sa'adya ben Joseph (882–942).

Born in Egypt, Sa'adya combined a keen intellect with a broad culture, so that he was able to keep in touch with the thought of the day and to use the new intellectual awakening in his own service in refuting the enemies of Judaism. It was in this way that he successfully turned the danger which threatened into an opportunity and a blessing. Arab conquest meant the spread of the Arab language, and it was not long before Arabic replaced the older Aramaic which had hitherto, for so long, served as the language both of the vernacular and of scholarship among the Jews. From now on, Arabic was the spoken tongue and soon became the medium for most literary activity; so that every learned Jew henceforth had to be master of three languages—the Hebrew of the Bible and the Mishna, Aramaic and Arabic. The near relationship between these three languages led to comparisons between them and thus the basis was laid for the science of philology, which was soon to be developed by Sa'adya and his successors to a very high level and used by them in the interpretation and explanation of the Scriptural text. Further, the efforts of learned Mohammedan scholars to effect a bridge between the Koran and contemporary philosophy induced Jewish teachers to do the same so far as the Bible was concerned. Thus, directly or indirectly, the advance of Islam opened new fields and wider horizons for Jewish Biblical commentary, and turned out to be a blessing in disguise.

In like manner, the Karaites also acted as a spur to a renewal of rabbinic literary activity in the exposition of the Bible—a task which might otherwise have been regarded as finished and closed. The Karaites are known in Hebrew as *Karaim* or, more usually *Bnei HaMikra*—followers of the written Biblical text. This sect came into being as a sort of reaction against the method of rabbinical interpretation which had become rooted in the great Academies of Babylon since the close of the Mishna and which had produced the Talmuds—a method devoted almost wholly to the discussion and development of the Oral Law. Long before this, in the Roman-Mishnaic days of the Second Temple, the Sadducees had tried to reject the tradition of the Oral Law and had insisted on the written word of Scripture. Now that same attitude was revived by the Karaites who, in the second half of the eighth century, led by a frustrated and disappointed man named Anan ben David, openly attacked the authority of the Rabbis and their talmudical interpretation and based themselves only on the Bible. The principle they laid down was "Search diligently in the Scripture"[22] so as to find therein all the laws for everyday life both for the individual and the community. The result was that they produced an atrophied Judaism—a religion that was harsh, cold, without the rabbinic understanding of the needs of the people or the rabbis' constant endeavour to find in tradition a means of alleviating stern legalisms. Moreover, none of the Karaite leaders was imbued with great originality and most of their work seems to have been inspired by the negative motive of attacking their rabbinic contemporaries. On the other hand, Karaism exerted a positive influence on Jewish Bible commentary not by its own achievements but by its reaction on rabbinical teachers who remained faithful to tradition.

By the time Sa'adya came on the scene, over a hundred years had elapsed since Anan and the Karaite sect had grown to measurable proportions, constituting a danger to be taken seriously. While quite a young man, his fame was established both by his literary work and by his part in a public controversy concerning the fixing of the Jewish calendar. Perhaps as a result of this, he was called to Babylon and appointed head of the School at Sura, with the title of Gaon. His absolute honesty and strong character soon led him into another controversy. He refused to sign a verdict given by the Exilarch in a probate case because he thought it unjust. When the Exilarch's son came again with the papers, Sa'adya told him to tell his father that the Torah teaches: "Thou shalt not respect persons in judgment." This led to open war, and Sa'adya was deposed and had to flee to Baghdad for about seven years before a reconciliation was effected and he was re-instated as Gaon of Sura. But those seven years in exile were full of activity by which Jewish thought was immeasurably enriched.

The versatility of his pen is particularly striking when it is remembered that he died at the young age of sixty, and that most of his writings were really pioneering. He contributed to nearly every field of Jewish study,—halacha, poetry, liturgy (he compiled the first *Siddur*), grammar (he was the first to write a Hebrew grammar and a dictionary of the Hebrew language), philology and philosophy. Abraham Ibn Ezra says of him that he was *Rosh Hamedabrim B'chol Makom*—"the chief speaker (teacher) in every place". But the chief occupation of his life was Biblical commentary. All his work centres round the Scriptures and the interpretation of the text. Thus his Grammar and his Dictionary were important because they introduced philology as a definite department of rabbinic scholarship and established a new method of Bible-study based on accurate scientific investigation of the text. Even his great philosophic work, *Emunot VeDe'ot* ('Beliefs and Opinions'), is based on the method of commenting on certain Scriptural passages. For every detail of his argument, he finds Biblical support. His major work in this field, however, was his Arabic translation of the Bible, which he called *TAFSIR*—a term denoting both translation and commentary combined. "If I am able," he writes in the Introduction, "to add therein a word or a letter which would make the matter and its purpose clear to a man of understanding ... I shall do so." In fact, he para-phrased only when he felt constrained to do so by the obscurity of the text; otherwise, the work is almost a word-for-word literal translation according to the *Peshat*. Since Arabic had become the language of the Jews of the East, Sa'adya recognised that the Hebrew Bible was a closed book to the majority of the people. Moreover, the Jews were no longer living a closed, self-contained life, cut off from con-tact with the outside world. On the contrary, intellectual influences from without were strong. His object in trans-lating the Bible into Arabic was therefore to make the Scriptures available and intelligible both to his own people and also to the world of Islam—just as the Septuagint had, many centuries earlier, brought the message of the Hebrew Bible to the Greek world. Sa'adya's translation, at all events, undoubtedly paved the way for the glorious Spanish Judaeo-Arabic period with all the fullness of its cultural blessing. Among the Jews of the East, it became hallowed in the same way as the earlier Targum of Onkelos, so that it was read together with the Hebrew text of each weekly portion of the Torah. Sa'adya intended his translation not for the scholarly but for the ordinary layman, Jew and non-Jew, and therefore he wrote it not merely in Arabic but also in Arabic characters. If he had had in mind only Jewish readers, he would have followed the more usual practice of using Hebrew characters. For the benefit of scholars, he wrote yet another translation—a very lengthy and detailed work, of which, however, only some portions have been preserved.

As the founder of the philological school of commentary, he frequently suggests an interpretation on the basis of the root meaning of the Hebrew word and a comparison between that word and a similar expression elsewhere. Often, however, his assumptions of possible meanings are arbitrary and have not been sustained by later commentators. Especially is this so in his translation of proper names of persons and places which are not explained in Scripture itself. Ibn Ezra later severely criticised Sa'adya for his insistence on translating these names; but he advanced a possible mitigating consideration, suggesting that perhaps Sa'adya did it out of consideration for the Mohammedans so that they should not be able to say that the Jews did not understand their own Bible (*Ibn Ezra* on *Gen.* 2. 11; 4. 19).

His philosophical approach, on the other hand, produced an interesting innovation in Jewish commentary. He was not content merely to render each word and sentence, but felt it necessary to write introductions to each whole book explaining the main issues and incidents in the book and the connection between them. Thus he treats each book as a unit calling for explanation and having a purpose of its own. Similarly, he is at great pains to eliminate anthropomorphisms, explaining them metaphorically or as figures of speech. For example, on the verse "And He (i.e. God) stood with him (Moses) there"—(Ex. 34. 5) he comments: "this means the Light which is called *Shechina*."[23]

Or again, the visions of God which the prophets beheld are explained as though God created some form out of light specially for the prophets so that they should understand that it was God Who was speaking to them; and this is what is referred to as 'The glory of the Lord', *Shechina*, or 'the angel of the Lord'. Similarly, where we are told that the prophets heard God's voice, we are not to understand that God has a voice which can be grasped by men, but that God on those occasions created a special sound or voice which only the prophets heard with *their* ears.

From the philosophical point of view, perhaps Sa'adya's greatest contribution lies in the fact that he was the first Jewish philosopher to appreciate the basic difference between the religious and the philosophic conceptions of truth; and, in the Introduction to his *Emunot VeDe'ot*, he emphasises the fact that Judaism is essentially and primarily a religion based on historical experience and that philosophy can only furnish secondary evidence of the worth of that experience and its teachings. Consequently he tries to give as literal a translation and version of the Scriptures as possible and he in fact lays down the rule that he can only permit himself to depart from the primary meaning of the text in four eventualities: When the face meaning of the text is in opposition (a) to human experience, or (b) to human intelligence; or (c) when two passages seem to contradict one another; or (d) when tradition seems to be opposed to the plain meaning of Scripture.

Let us now see one or two examples of his style. On the verse "For the Lord thy God is a devouring fire"—(Deut. 4. 24), he comments:

"the meaning is that He is *like* a devouring fire. And I find that the language does admit of comparisons without using the letter *Kaph* ('like'), as, for instance, 'And He brought you forth from the iron furnace'—(Deut. 4. 20) where the meaning is '*like* from the iron furnace'; So also *a devouring fire* means to say, *He is like a devouring fire*— which denotes a punishment."[24]

And on the verse: "For the blood is the soul (or *life*)"— (Deut. 12. 23) he adds:

"the blood is its abode and its centre. ... And when the soul is joyful ... the blood rejoices with it, and when it flees because it is afraid of something, it draws the blood with it inwards. And as to what the Torah said that the blood *is* the soul, that is only because of the style of the language which calls an object after its abode; just as it uses the word *heart* (lev) to mean *wisdom* when it says

(Prov. 7. 7): *A young man is devoid of wisdom*, because understanding resides in the heart."[25]

Incidentally, this comment was most probably directed against the Karaite founder, Anan, who, taking the literal meaning of the verse, held that the blood was in fact the substance of the soul. But Sa'adya, in his Arabic translation, pointed to another verse (Lev. 17. 11): "For the soul of the flesh is in the blood",—and consequently maintained that the soul lives and reveals itself *in* the blood, but is not identical with it. (See P. R. Weiss, article in *Sa'adya Studies*, Manchester 1943.) Again, on an important matter of penal law, the Karaites took the verse, *An eye for an eye* (Ex. 21. 24; Deut. 19. 21) literally as *Lex Talionis*; while Sa'adya interpreted it, in conformity with Jewish tradition, to mean a money indemnity or compensation.

The lustre which Sa'adya's brilliance shed upon the great School at Sura hardly outlived the Gaon himself. The famous Academies of learning in Babylon were already on the decline and the centre of Jewish life was beginning to move away from the East. The creative work of Babylonian Jewry was done and its achievements were soon to pass on as a heritage to the communities of the West. It was there, especially in the new Schools of North Africa and Spain, that Sa'adya's influence continued to be felt; and, nearly two hundred years after his death, another luminary, R. Bachaye, said of his books on Scripture that: "they illumined the intelligence and sharpened the understanding".[26] (Introduction to *Chovat Halevavot.*) Not only was he successful in preventing the spread of Karaism with its deadly schismatic effects, but, through his endeavours to harmonise Jewish belief with the new Moslem culture, he set the course for subsequent scholars for the next three centuries during which Jews were to live in Arab lands.

8

The Medieval Philosophers

THE SPREAD of Islam and of Arab dominion brought a measure of relief to the Jews in the early Middle Ages. When the empire that had been founded by help of the Koran and the sword was firmly established, the sword was put aside and the Caliphs decided to maintain their ascendancy by the arts of peace rather than by war. They aimed at becoming leaders of men and patrons of learning; they wanted the arts of civilisation to adorn their lands. To this end the Arab rulers cultivated their Jewish subjects, who were granted political and social equality. By the tenth century, the Moslem empire had become very extensive and had three main centres of government—at Baghdad, Cairo, and Cordova in Southern Spain. At about this time, too, the Jewish schools of learning in Babylon were closed and the seat and centre of Jewish life and letters moved to the West—especially to the sunshine and liberty of Spain. Jewish writers of those days refer to their new land of adoption as 'an earthly paradise', 'a garden of Eden'; and so it continued until about the middle of the twelfth century when part of Spain returned to Christian rule and the Arab lands also came under the hand of a new dynasty—the Almohades—at once barbarian and ruthlessly conversionist in policy. But the few hundred years of peace, of tolerance, of friendship and of the patronage of learning, had produced a most fruitful impact of Judaism and Islamic thought on one another. In particular, there developed at this time, among the Jews of Spain, a strong philosophic movement as a result of the need to reconcile Scripture teaching with the new truths of the age. The world of Jewish tradition was up against a challenge, the challenge of a new foreign culture; and, just as the Greek period had called forth the Jewish Hellenistic thought in Palestine and Egypt, so now again Jewish philosophers and commentators arose in Spain who saw it as their duty to vindicate the truth of Jewish teaching.

Now the philosophy which was current at that time was Greek in origin and "the Jews were the pupils of the Arabs and followed their lead in adapting Greek thought to their own intellectual and spiritual needs" (Husik: *History of Mediaeval Jewish Philosophy*, p. xx). But this Greek thought, in the form of neo-platonism, was essentially rationalistic— that is, based on the acceptance of human intellect and reasoning as the supreme judge and arbiter of truth; and as such it was naturally opposed to the fundamental outlook of Scripture, which was based on faith. The rationalistic standpoint was really strange to the spirit of the Bible and traditional Judaism, where the basic outlook is that God and His Will are supreme and often beyond human comprehension.

From the time of Sa'adya Gaon onwards, Jewish thinkers acquired the new philosophical rationalistic mode of thought and were convinced of its rightness. But, at the same time, they believed with all their hearts in the teachings of the Bible and Jewish tradition and so their work represents a constant attempt to attune the one to the other. And it must be admitted that their efforts to reconcile seeming contradictions sometimes led them to give a somewhat forced explanation to the words of Scripture, far different from their literal face-meaning.

The first of this line of Spanish-Jewish philosophers was Solomon Ibn Gabirol (1020–1070), whose fame to this day

51

rests mainly on his merit as a celebrated poet. As a philosopher, he was neglected by succeeding generations, and his chief work, the *Mekor Chayim* (or "Fountain of Life"), was, in the course of time, quite forgotten. The Arabic original was lost and there was no Hebrew translation. On the other hand, it was translated into Latin by Christian scholars, and the name of Gabirol as its author was lost until the nineteenth century. The "Fountain of Life" in fact, was not looked upon kindly by other medieval Jewish scholars because it makes no attempt to reconcile religion with philosophy. In this, Gabirol was quite outstanding and distinctive. He nowhere quotes a Biblical verse or a talmudical teaching. And yet we have evidence that this philosopher-poet also occupied himself considerably with Biblical commentary and several examples of his approach are quoted by Ibn Ezra, who gives them in the name of "Rabbi Solomon the Spaniard, the author of weighty poetry". His style was allegorical. Eden, he says, means the upper world, and the Garden represents the world of angelic beings. Adam is the rational soul; Eve, the animal soul; and the serpent is the soul of the appetite. The serpent entices Adam to eat the fruit of the forbidden tree. This means that when the lower soul succeeds in controlling reason, the result is evil and sin, and man is driven out of his state of angelic purity. He also supports the rationalistic approach of Sa'adya in maintaining that the Serpent (in the Genesis story) and the ass (in the episode with Balaam) did not speak, but that an angel was made to speak for them. We do not know what were the sources of Ibn Ezra's quotations of Gabirol's comments. No specific work of Biblical commentary has come down to us from Gabirol. But, from the gleaned references to his method, it seems that he deliberately kept Jewish religious teaching out of his "Fountain of Life" because of his view that philosophy and religion or theology should be kept apart in a book on philosophy. The harmonising of the two was an important task—but one which should be reserved for the field of Biblical commentary.

Quite different, and in a class by himself, was the other great poet and philosopher, Yehuda Halevi, who was born, in Toledo, about the time of Gabirol's death or a little after. Yehuda Halevi will chiefly be remembered as the Jewish poet-laureate of the Middle Ages, and his poetry, permeated with nationalist longing and religious fervour, is permanently enshrined among the spiritual treasures of the Jewish people. Indeed, in him the poet rose above the rationalist, and his great philosophical treatise, the *Kuzari*, represents a strong protest against the rationalist approach to Biblical exposition. He stood out against all those who, since Sa'adya Gaon, had tried to explain Scripture in terms of their philosophy and rational understanding. The Torah, he concedes, does not contain anything which controverts that which can be proved by logic or mathematics. There is nothing in Scripture which opposes reason and scientific proof:

> "Heaven forbid that there should be anything in the Bible to contradict that which is manifest or proved!" —(*Kuz*. I. 67).[27]

But reason and knowledge alone, he says, are not enough to enable us to grasp the truths of Judaism and the nature of God. These have to be approached with love, and not with arguments of logic, and the key to this comprehension is revelation. Scripture does not depend on rational proofs, but on a much stronger support, namely, the long line of living tradition and historical experience of the people of Israel who had a personal knowledge of God at Sinai. Therefore, the Bible cannot be judged on the basis of human outlook, for "it belongs to the province of the

Divine influence, not to that of the intellectual, human or natural world."[28] So also the Jewish people is not to be judged like other nations, because there is a peculiar relation between God and Israel in which other peoples do not share. The proper way to define religion is not by argument but by tradition and experience which are more reliable. The Jewish people has this very experience; for it is well known that the God of Abraham, Isaac and Jacob spoke to Moses and delivered the Children of Israel from Egypt, and gave them the Torah. Other peoples who accept the knowledge of God will also be rewarded, but they are not equal to Israel. Similarly he ascribes a special holiness to the Land of Israel which was set aside for the ultimate working out of God's design. In short, Yehuda Halevi deliberately affirms that Scripture is high above all philosophic rationalisation and not in any way in need of it or dependent upon it. In contrast to Maimonides, he did not have anything like the same degree of respect for the possibilities of human reason, which he regarded as fallible and subject to differences of opinion. As against this, he had a far greater respect for the traditional teachings of Judaism and thus he saw no need to twist the plain *Peshat* or face-meaning of the Biblical text.

The key to the understanding of Halevi's almost mystical fundamentalist outlook is in his ardent nationalism. In his philosophy, in his approach to religion and the Bible, he is as strongly patriotic as in his poetry. In his day, the cloud began to appear on the Spanish horizon and though it was no bigger than a man's hand and while he himself was still received in court circles and prospered, he felt that his people were once more on the defensive. It was this which strengthened his native Jewish nationalistic fervour and called forth the expression of his intense love for his people and his people's land which led him eventually to leave his friends and the place of his fame and glory and journey to

Palestine, where, according to legend, he was pierced through with the spear of an Arab horseman as he was singing his famous Ode to Zion. Throughout his *Kuzari*, Yehuda Halevi is conscious that he is "defending a persecuted race and a despised faith against not merely the philosophers but against the more powerful and more fortunate professors of other religions. He is the loyal son of his race and his religion, and he *will* show that they are above all criticism, that they are the best and the truest there are. ... ...Yehuda Halevi takes the stand of one who fights for his hearth and home against the attacks of foreign foes. He will not yield an inch to the adversary." (Husik.) With him, it is not merely a question of finding an inner balance between Judaism and philosophy, or between Scripture and rationalism. Rather is it a case of having to defend his Judaism against external attack. Thus he begins his *Kuzari* with the words: "I was asked to state what arguments and replies I could bring to bear against the attacks of philosophers and followers of other religions. ..."

★　　★　　★　　★　　★

The summit of medieval Jewish philosophy was attained in the life and work of Moses Maimonides. No other Jewish teacher exercised such an influence as he did both on his own generation and on posterity. Whereas Yehuda Halevi had been motivated by unquestioned faith and held that acceptance of the Bible was above reason, Maimonides' intellectual labours were devoted to seeking harmony between faith and reason. He was essentially the rationalist seeking to reconcile his Judaism with philosophy in an age when philosophy was in the air and when many religionists (Jews and others) were becoming alarmed at its progress.

Born in Cordova in 1135, his boyhood was spent in an

unsettled environment. "The Koran or the Sword" had by now become the rule; and neither Jew nor Christian could openly avow his faith. The Maimon family decided to leave Spain and finally they settled in Egypt. Moses became famed both as a physician and for his rabbinic scholarship; and soon he was the spiritual head of the Jews of Egypt and the guide and adviser to Jews in other lands. He always felt closer to Islam than to Christianity. In his famous Arabic letter known as the *Iggeret Hash'mad* (Letter concerning Apostasy) which he addressed to the Jews living in Moslem lands, where they were forced to declare the formula of submission to Islam, he wrote: "Any Jew who, after uttering the Moslem formula, wishes to observe the whole six hundred and thirteen precepts in the privacy of his home, may do so without hindrance. ..." Another of his famous letters is the *Iggeret Teman* (Letter to the South) addressed to the Jews of Yemen when they too were suddenly threatened with apostasy or martyrdom.

Maimonides, however, is best known for his two major works, the *Yad Hachazaka* (or *Mishne Torah*), and the *More Nevuchim* ('Guide to the Perplexed'). The *Mishne Torah* was a new codification of Jewish law; but it produced a conflict which raged for a hundred years. Maimonides stood for a combination of Jewish religious tradition with current scientific knowledge—which meant, in effect, with Aristotelian philosophy. But orthodox circles demurred. It was, however, in the *Guide* that Maimonides undertook the specific task of reconciling Faith with Reason. Intended originally only for a small circle of disciples, it became widely known only after his death through being translated into Hebrew by Samuel Ibn Tibbon.

Using the phrase in Proverbs 25. 11,—"apples of gold in settings of silver"—Maimonides held that the words of Scripture can have two meanings—the revealed and the hidden. The revealed, i.e. the *Peshat*, is as silver,—he explains in the Introduction to the *Guide*—but "its inner meaning is better than the revealed, as gold is more valuable than silver. This is how it is with the parables, for instance, of the prophets; their plain revealed surface meaning is helpful for ordering human society, while their inner, hidden wisdom leads us to the true Faith." The hidden meaning is the essential and more important of the two, but it does not contradict or deny the revealed meaning. For instance, when God says to Moses "behold there is a place by Me and thou shalt stand on the rock,"—(Ex. 33. 21.)—we are to understand from this: "that God wanted Moses to attain to a degree of divine or prophetic insight and comprehension, and not simply a place visible to the eye";[29] but this is linked with the revealed meaning, namely "the actual place shown to him where he would have solitude and thereby attain that degree of perfection."[30] Similarly Maimonides also seeks to explain the miracles in rationalistic fashion so as to uphold the literal meaning of the text without contradicting the philosophical teaching concerning the fixed laws of nature. The miracles, he asserts, really took place as related in Scripture, and yet they were not in opposition to the fixed laws of nature; for when God fixed the laws of nature for all eternity, He at the same time determined that they should change at those certain given moments and circumstances mentioned in Scripture. And the prophets who foretold the miracles knew, by the divine spirit of prophecy, that the laws of nature were due to be altered as preordained by God at the time of Creation (*Guide*, 2. 29). Even the very faculty of prophecy itself is thought by Maimonides to be obtainable (at least in part) by moral and intellectual development to a very high degree.

The *Guide for the Perplexed* is full of quotations from Scripture, and whole sections are devoted to philosophical explanations of Biblical incidents, chapters, and even whole books. Maimonides became the acknowledged leader of those who thought they could read Aristotelian metaphysics into the sacred Scriptures, and his influence was stamped on Jewish and Christian scholars for generations afterwards.

9

Rashi

WHILE THE golden age of Spanish Jewry was at its zenith, there seems to have been little or no contact at all with the neighbouring Jews of France, especially of Northern France. This is not really surprising when we bear in mind the difficulties of communication generally in the Middle Ages, as well as the fact that France was Christian while Spain was mainly Moslem. In southern France, or Provence, matters were rather different, for this area constituted a separate cultural entity or unit much more closely connected with the cultural life of the Jews of Spain. But northern France and Germany comprised quite another world and the Jews there reflected the different influences in their own life and thought. In Spain the Jews lived a full and free life, basking in the sunshine of Islamic civilisation in its finest hour, writing poetry, studying philology, grammar, mathematics and philosophy, and generally taking their part in the development of a many-sided culture. All this was naturally reflected in their literary work, and we have seen how Arabic philology and, above all, the new awakening to Greek philosophy, through Arabic translations, made their tremendous impact on Jewish religious teaching, and particularly on Biblical interpretation.

None of these influences or conditions were present in France of those days. There the Jews lived hemmed in by restrictions and bigotry and surrounded by simple, uneducated Christian peasants. Such learning as did exist was confined to the clergy, with whom the Jews had nothing in common and from whom they, as a rule, deemed it prudent to keep at a safe distance. Moreover, they knew no Arabic and were thus cut off from the rich Hebrew-Arabic literature. They were essentially French in outlook, and when one remembers that these were the days of pre-Renaissance Europe, in the so-called Dark Ages, one can better appreciate the enormously important rôle which the Jews' own religious and literary sources played in preserving their own standards of life and learning. They were forced to devote their undivided attention to the Bible and the Talmud and because they gave themselves to fewer subjects they delved into them all the more deeply. Their exposition of the text of their precious sources was wholly Jewish, without any admixture of foreign influences from the outside. It was based entirely upon ancient midrashic and mishnaic teaching, on the views of the Sages of the Talmud, on the traditional Aramaic Targumim and on the Massora; for, in contrast to the Jews in Moslem lands, they had nothing to learn from their neighbours, and their only support was the culture of Jewish tradition.

For a long time, the Jews of France and Germany ('Ashkenaz' Jews, they came to be called, in contrast to the 'Sepharad' Jews or 'Sephardim', meaning the Jews of Spain) looked to the great Schools of Sura and Pumbedita for instruction and guidance; but at the end of the tenth century a new school, which was soon to become the centre of inspiration for the Jews of all Christian Europe, was established at Mayence by Rabbi Gershom, and it was this school which shortly produced the most famous and the most popular of all Jewish commentators, RASHI. There is a midrashic dictum which runs, "when one star sets in Israel, another star rises on the horizon". In the very year when the great Babylonian Academies were closed (1040) Rashi was born in far away Troyes, in France. His name really was Rabbi *Shelomo* bar *Isaac*, and it is the initial letters of those words which make the name *Rashi*. Little is known of his life except that he studied under disciples of Rabbenu Gershom at Worms and Mayence, and then returned to his native Troyes where he remained until his death in 1105, teaching, gathering disciples and earning his meagre livelihood by manual work in the vineyards. For more than thirty years, Rashi taught the Bible and the Talmud, going systematically through each book, explaining and clarifying every difficult point in the text. It is these explanations which eventually formed the material for his great works, his monumental Commentaries on nearly all the books of the Bible and on almost the whole of the Talmud.

Rashi's aim is to enable the reader to obtain a clear understanding of the text. He is not interested in criticisms of what is in the text; nor is he concerned with apologetics. He does not examine any book as a whole; and he has not contributed introductions, prefaces or other essays setting forth his theological or philosophical views. His method is that of the running commentary, explaining the meaning of the text as he goes along, word for word and verse by verse. With other members of his school—especially some of his eminent disciples and successors—he sets out to give the plain, unembellished meaning, the *Peshat*; and yet his commentary is a mine of midrashic material also. The natural tendency towards the *Peshat* no doubt had something to do with the close attention that was paid to the teaching of the Talmud, which these teachers regarded as a special responsibility now that the Babylonian centres were no more. Rashi was, in a way, a successor to the Geonim, and was called upon to examine the Talmud text from the point of view of extracting the *Halacha Le Ma'ase*—practical legal decisions. And as Talmud and Scripture were regarded as merely two parts of one Torah, the *Peshat* approach to the Talmud was naturally also applied to the exposition of the Bible. He is terse, and sparing in the use of words. He goes right to the point; while his incredibly retentive memory enables him continually to base his note on older rabbinic teachings. On the verse (Deut. 19. 18): "And behold if the witness be a false witness," Rashi notes:—

"Wherever the word *witness* is written, Scripture is referring (unless otherwise explicitly stated) to *two* witnesses."

Or, to take another instance, on the verse (Lev. 19. 18): *Lo Tikkom V'lo Tittor*, "Thou shalt not *take vengeance* nor *bear a grudge* ...*", he explains the distinction between the two as follows:

"If one says to another, Lend me thy sickle, and he replies, No! and the next day the latter says to the former: Lend me thy hatchet, and he retorts: No, I shall not, because thou didst refuse me yesterday;—that is avenging. And what is 'bearing grudge'? If one says to another: Lend me thy hatchet, and he replies, No!, and the next day the latter says to the former: Lend me thy sickle, and he says: Here it is, for I am not like thee who wouldst not lend me;—that is 'bearing a grudge', because he retains the enmity in his heart although he does not avenge himself."

In both the above cases, Rashi is giving the meaning of the text according to the teaching of the Talmud, but with such directness and simplicity that he who runs may read. His simple language and style made the Bible an open book to laymen and children, and earned him the title *Parshandata*— *the* interpreter par excellence.

Often, his desire for the straightforward sense of the text leads him to reject the midrashim of the early Sages. For instance, the statement in Genesis (4. 8): "And Cain said to

Abel his brother ..." calls forth Rashi's explanation as follows:—

"He began an argument, striving and contending with him." And then he adds: "there are midrashic explanations of these words, but this is the real, plain sense of the text."

Similarly, he comments on Zech. 1. 8:

"Our fathers explained what they explained. ... But the sequence of the portion and its language do not tally with it ..."[31]

At the same time, Rashi often did use midrashim, too, in seeking to give a reasonable explanation of the text, but then he was invariably at pains to find the midrash which seemed to him to be closest to the *Peshat*. Thus, in the account of Adam and Eve, where the verse says: "And they heard the voice of the Lord God walking about in the garden ..."— (Gen. 3. 8), Rashi says:—

"There are many midrashic explanations. ... I, however, am only concerned with the plain sense of Scripture and with such Agadot that explain the words of Scripture in a manner that fits in with them."

Indeed, there are several midrashic explanations which Rashi understood as themselves giving the plain literal sense, and that is why he so frequently quotes them. "Rashi", says Liber in his monograph (p. 124), "not only popularised numerous midrashim, but he also preserved a number, the sources of which are no longer extant, and which, without him, would be unknown. His Biblical Commentary is thus the store-house of midrashic literature." Sometimes, he even uses a midrashic explanation when he feels it to be not in harmony with the *Peshat*— simply because he cannot find a better comment, as on the verse (Gen. 25. 22): "And the children struggled together within her (Rebecca)"—where Rashi adds:—

> "Perforce this verse calls for a midrashic interpretation since it leaves unexplained what the struggling was about ..."

And often when he does not accept the traditional midrashic explanations, he still does not reject them, but offers them as a possible alternative. Thus after giving his own direct interpretation of the words: "And he erected there an altar and called it El-Elohe-Yisrael" (Gen. 33. 20), he adds: "But our rabbis expounded it to mean that the Holy One, blessed be He, called Jacob by the name El. However the words of the Torah may be given many different explanations, just as a hammer splits the rock into many different pieces. But *I* make it my aim to give the plain sense of Scripture."

In keeping with his main objective, Rashi gave considerable and frequent attention to grammar in order to get at the right meaning of a word. Out of touch as he was with the field of Arabic literature, he was at a handicap and was forced to do some pioneering. However, two earlier Spanish grammarians had written in the Hebrew language. They were Menachem ben Saruk and Dunash ibn Labrat. Rashi knew their works and often quotes them, even when he does not agree with them.

An interesting oddity in Rashi's commentaries is his frequent translation of a difficult word into the French vernacular of his day which he called *loaz*. There have been suggestions that this word stands for *Lashon Am Zar*—"the language of a strange people;" but more probably it is simply the word found in Ps. 114. 1—

> "When Israel went forth from Egypt, the house of Jacob from a people of a *strange language*" (*Me'Am Loez*).

These French glosses or *loazim*, as they are called, number over three thousand, and are, incidentally, of great importance in reconstructing the Old French language from which modern French is descended.

Rashi's grandson, Rabbi Shmuel ben Meir (called popularly *Rashbam*), in his commentary on Gen. 37. 2, makes this illuminating reference to his illustrious grandfather:—

> "And I ... had discussions and arguments with him, and he admitted to me that if he had had the leisure he would have deemed it necessary to rewrite his Commentaries in accordance with modern literal interpretations."[32]

This is just another example of the modesty of the man and a measure of his greatness and open-mindedness in constantly searching after the truth. After him, other Rabbis—among them his own three grandsons and other members of his family—made additions—(*Tosaphot*)—to his comments and glosses; but Rashi's own commentaries have remained to this day the most important and indispensable key to the understanding of the Bible and the Talmud. So valuable was his work thought to be and so permanent its influence, that when, in 1475, the first Hebrew book ever to be printed appeared in Italy, it was an edition of Rashi's commentary to the Pentateuch.

10

Abraham Ibn Ezra

THE MIDDLE of the twelfth century marks the beginning of the decline in the condition of Spanish Jewry. The almost idyllic circumstances in which they had lived for about two and a half centuries were sharply interrupted and, within a short time, great and famous centres of Judaism were destroyed. Refugee scholars, fleeing from the threat of murder or apostasy, found their way to Christian northern Spain or to other Christian lands, where they sought a temporary foothold; and the change in the fortunes of these people made it imperative to find some way of rescuing and preserving for future generations the spiritual treasures that had been stored up in Arab lands and under Moslem influence since the time of Sa'adya. This applied particularly to the extensive and many-sided field of Biblical commentary, which had by now grown to such sizeable proportions. Fortunately, the period was blessed with the ideal man for this task, Abraham ben Meir Ibn Ezra (1092–1167).

A younger contemporary of his, Ibn Daud, speaks of him as the last of those who formed the pride of Spanish Judaism and who "strengthened the hands of Israel with songs and with words of comfort." He spent the first half of his life in his native Toledo; when he was nearly fifty, he took the wanderer's staff in his hand and became a roving scholar. No doubt there were several factors which led him to this course. First, as we have just noted, Jewish life was no longer so easy in Southern Spain. Secondly, he appears to have lived in poverty. With his characteristic humour, he said of himself: "I strive to become wealthy but the stars are against me. If I were to make shrouds I am sure people would stop dying; or if I were to follow the trade of making candles, the sun would never set." A third reason is connected with a tragic event in his life, namely the conversion of his son, Israel, to Islam, and it has been suggested that the father went abroad with his son in the hope of being able to win him back to Judaism. In this, however, he was not successful, and, lonely and grief-stricken, he wandered on to Rome in 1140, after he had visited Africa, Egypt, Palestine and Babylon. Up till now, he had shown very little of his literary talents and in Spain he seems to have been known only as a poet. In the Introduction to his later commentary on the Torah, he refers to himself as *Ha-Shar*—"The Poet"; and elsewhere he says: "Once in my youth I used to compose songs with which I decorated the Hebrew scholars as with a necklace." But all the time he was storing up knowledge which showed itself in his later abundant writings.

He remained a rolling stone to the end of his days. Though he found peace in Italy, he nevertheless moved about from Rome to Lucca, Mantua and Verona. He also spent some years in France, and even went on to London in his seventieth year. In all these places, he says, "I resided as a stranger, wrote books, and revealed the secrets of knowledge." Regarding himself as an exile, he makes repeated touching references to Spain and always calls himself "Spaniard" (*Sepharadi*). Wherever he went he was constantly busy writing; and as he wrote in Hebrew, he obviously worked with the set purpose of bringing the enlightenment and learning of Spain to the non-Arabic speaking Jews of Christian Europe. With astounding versatility, he wrote books on astronomy, grammar, philosophy and poetry, and generally propagated the scientific and rationalistic spirit as it had been developed, in Jew and Arab alike,

in Spain. His importance lies chiefly, however, in his Biblical commentary which not only summarizes the earlier
works in this field written in Arabic, but also, in a wonderful
Hebrew, forms its epitome. It is a mine of information, with
quotations from, and references to, ever so many of Ibn
Ezra's forerunners,—Rabbanites and Karaites, the Geonim
and the philosophers—sometimes using them as support for
his own views and sometimes differing from them sharply
and, now and then, even contemptuously, with a vitriolic pen.

Approaching his task in a scientific manner he analyses, in
the Introduction to his Commentary on the Torah, four
methods of Bible exposition that had been used by others
and which he finds it necessary to reject. First, there is the
approach of the Geonim (notably Sa'adya) who, he feels,
introduced into their commentaries much unnecessary
material derived from secular, foreign learning, and not
directly touching on the understanding of the text. This had
made their expositions too long—

> "And there is no benefit in this sort of commentary
> except its length;"[33]

> "and those who wish to devote themselves to external
> wisdom should learn it from the books of men of (secular)
> understanding."[34]

Secondly, he attacks the method of the Karaites who
thought they could understand the Scriptures without the
aid of tradition as preserved in the work of the Scribes, the
Mishna and the Talmud. There are many commandments
in the Torah, he says, which could not be understood at all
without the traditions of the early Sages. The Written Law
and the Oral Law are both ultimately derived from one and
the same authority—namely, the chain of living tradition
as handed down from generation to generation:—

"For there is no difference between the two Torahs; both are ours by tradition from our fathers."[35]

"For from our fathers we received the Written Torah also, just as we heard the Oral Law from their mouths. And if the Oral Law is not true, then likewise there can be no healing in the Written Torah either."[36]

Thirdly, Ibn Ezra is opposed to the allegorical method that some had used in explaining Scripture. This, he says, is

"the way of the uncircumcised who say that the whole Torah consists of allegories and parables."

This is a dangerous method, for, he explains—

"Everyone interprets according to his own ideas according to the perception of his own mind; one adding, another diminishing, sometimes for better and sometimes for worse."

Here Ibn Ezra is particularly attacking the method adopted by Christian scholars who had always sought to give a so-called 'spiritualised' interpretation of the text; and after mentioning a number of examples of this Christian allegorical interpretation, he adds:

"All these words are void—driven vanity, such that there is nothing to compare with it."[37]

Finally, he takes to task those Jewish commentators in Christian lands who pay no heed to the grammar of the Hebrew tongue, but rely only on collections of diverse midrashim which, he says, were never intended by the Sages to be understood as giving the sense of the Bible text.
As for his own method—

"this is the fifth method, the foundation of my own

personal commentary, to explain every text according to the verse, the grammar and the literal meaning."

He is prepared to make use of the midrashic literature whenever it fits the language of the text, but where the midrashic explanation seems forced, he prefers to follow the plain, obvious sense of the words of the text; for in such cases, the midrash is only—

"an aid to the memory and a general support; but they (the Sages) knew well the *Peshat*, for all wisdom was given to them."[38]

Ibn Ezra's aim was to make the text clear in a simple, natural, reasonable way, in much the same manner as that in which Rashi had written half a century earlier. But Rashi had added much fanciful midrashic material, and of this Ibn Ezra disapproved, especially when he saw it carried to inordinate lengths by Rashi's successors.

One of the most striking things about Ibn Ezra and his commentaries is the boldness, the courage and independence which are in evidence throughout. It must have taken all these qualities to enable him to attack a Sa'adya and to reject midrashic interpretations that were widely accepted; and he never faltered even in the face of criticism:

"God alone will I fear, and I will not pretend (or show favour) with regard to the Torah."[39]

It was this independence of spirit and critical mind always searching for the truth that made him known as the first Jewish Bible critic. Thus he dared to suggest—though only vaguely and in a way that would be understood only by the more select circle of the pious and learned, and not by all and sundry—that certain passages in the Torah were written not by Moses, but by others. For example, he thought that the account of the death of Moses in Deuteronomy chapter 34 was written by Joshua; and he was probably the first Jewish scholar to hold the view that the last twenty six chapters of Isaiah were written by a later, second Isaiah who lived and taught in the Babylonian exile.

Ibn Ezra's independent spirit is reflected not only in the content of his work, but also in his style. He was one who could not suffer fools gladly; he had a biting wit; he hated shallowness and dilletantism; and he was no respecter of persons. His versified style is curt, strictly to the point, often playful and humorous, and full of allusions, delighting and rewarding the careful reader. Because of the richness of the Hebrew style, it is particularly difficult to convey its significance in a translation; but one or two examples may give something of his approach. Thus on Ex. 21. 35, "If a man's ox gore the ox of his neighbour," he says:

"Ben Zota says that the word *Re'ehu* is a description of the ox. ... But an ox has no *Re'a* (lit. a 'friend') except Ben Zota himself."[40]

Again, on Gen. 9. 27—

"God enlarge Japhet"—

he says that Sa'adya Gaon—

"explained the word *yaft* as if it were from the root *yafa*, but his explanation is not *yafe*—'beautiful',"

On the word *Edadem* in Psalms 42. 5, he attacks the pioneer grammarian Ibn Labrat with another play on words:—

"Ibn Labrat says that the word *Edadem* is a doubled form of the same root as 'Edom'. Would that he would be silent (*Ve Yidom*)!"[41]

We have already observed how much Abraham Ibn Ezra

missed his native Spain. At the age of seventy five, it seems that he determined to return there, but he died on the way, at Calahorra, on the borders of Navarre and Aragon. Even on his death-bed, his old habit of punning did not leave him, for it is reported that, among his last words, he wittily applied to himself the verse from Genesis (12. 4): "And Abraham was seventy five years old when he departed from the wrath of this world"—reading *Charan* (the city's name) as if it were *Charon* (wrath).

11

The Kimchi Family

THE DECLINE in the position of Spanish Jewry, after the middle of the twelfth century, led to the move of several scholars northwards towards France and other Christian countries. Ibn Ezra was thus driven to leave his native Toledo in the south and become a wandering scholar, carrying his learning to many lands. Others, however, were content to take one step, as it were, beyond the borders of Spain and settle down in the sunny, more liberal and care-free Provence, the wealthiest portion of France. Here, in an atmosphere of gaiety and troubadour poetry, the Jews found ample opportunity not only to engage in business, but also to develop a very broad mental horizon, liberal, free from bigotry, combining at once the talmudic acumen of the north with the more worldly culture of Spain. Provence became, in fact, a bridge between the two centres of Jewish life and its scholars became the carriers of the now waning Arab-Jewish thought and civilisation into the heart of Europe.

Until now, Arabic had been the language most prevalent among Jewish scholars—as indeed it was the language normally spoken at least throughout the Mediterranean region. Any writer who wanted to make an impression wrote, therefore, perforce in Arabic; and this applied, for instance, to such important works as the *Guide for the Perplexed* and the *Mishna Commentary* of Maimonides, the *Kuzari* of Yehuda Halevi, and others. Now, however, with the shadows closing in upon the Arabic stream of civilisation, it became necessary to save these works from oblivion and a

73

new genre of literary activity arose, namely, the art of translation from the Arabic originals into pure Hebrew. Most famous of the translators was the family of Ibn Tibbon, who formed part of the côterie of intellectuals who gathered in the city of Lunel. Judah Ibn Tibbon, who came to Lunel because of the persecutions in his native Spain, translated Halevi's *Kuzari*, Sa'adya's *Emunot Vede'ot*, as well as the poems of Ibn Gabirol, and earned the title 'father of translators'; while his son, Samuel, was the translator, as we have seen, of Maimonides' *Guide*. Moreover, Samuel Ibn Tibbon later translated into Hebrew other classical works, like those of Aristotle and Averroes, which had been known and used in Spain in Arabic versions. These translations proved subsequently to be of immense consequence, for they were the medium by which much of this classical literature was passed on to medieval Christendom where both Greek and Arabic were then unknown. It was through Latin retranslations from these new Hebrew versions that the treasures of ancient Greece began to spread among the scholars of the European world, planting the seeds of the eventual Renaissance.

Forming part of this intellectual setting, and contributing richly to its fulness, was another family whose name has become famous in the history of Jewish letters. This was the Kimchi family, famed not only as translators but even more particularly as grammarians and commentators. The father of this family, Joseph Kimchi, was born in southern Spain in 1105, but later, to escape persecution, moved to the Provençal city of Narbonne, where he died in 1170. He was thus a contemporary of Ibn Ezra who quotes him in his commentaries. Their common purpose was to make the Arabic-Jewish works available, in Hebrew translations, to the Jews of Europe.

Joseph's older son, Moses Kimchi, (known in Hebrew as

ReMaK) wrote commentaries to several books of the Bible; but they were so much influenced by Ibn Ezra that they have often been attributed to him. Among his works was a concise, methodical text-book of Hebrew grammar which was later translated into Latin and published in several editions, being used extensively by non-Jews in the sixteenth century. But the greatest of the family was the younger son, David, (*ReDaK*) who, born in Narbonne in 1160, was virtually brought up by his elder brother. David, too, wrote a Hebrew Grammar and also a Dictionary, *Sefer HaSharashim* —'The Book of Roots'—which, in its turn, greatly influenced later Christian works. As a Bible commentator, his popularity ranks second perhaps only to that of Rashi; while for Christian scholars he was possibly of the first importance. Numerous Latin translations were made of his commentaries and were widely studied by Christian Hebraists in the period of the revival of learning in the sixteenth century; so that, indirectly, these works of *ReDaK* profoundly influenced the first English version of the Bible published in 1611—the King James' Bible, Authorized Version.

One modern scholar, Jacob Bosniak, in the Introduction to his critical edition of David Kimchi's Commentary to the fifth book of Psalms, stresses the fact that *ReDaK* enjoyed great popularity in his own lifetime as a *Darshan*—a Preacher, or Teacher; that he was not merely an exegete, but a public expounder of the Scriptures who was at pains to make the text understood by his audiences; and that this influenced his style, which is often repetitious and lengthy, and led him to comment on many verses which seem hardly to call for elucidation. The most popular of his commentaries seems to have been that on Psalms, for it was in connection with this work that it was said of him, playing on the words of the Mishna *Pirke Avot*, "If there is no *Kemach* (lit. 'flour'—i.e. bread—but here meaning Kimchi) there is no Torah"—that is, one cannot understand Scripture with out Kimchi's interpretations. In his exposition of the text, he makes frequent reference to contemporary events, especially as they affected the life of the Jews in the medieval world. Thus on Psalms 120. 2, he says,

> "So do we suffer among the nations where we find our-selves, for they are false and deceitful;"

and again, on the verse, *Pray for the peace of Jerusalem* (Ps. 122. 6), he makes reference to the Wars of the Crusades,

> "For until now she (Jerusalem) had no peace, for the uncircumcised (i.e. the Christians) and the Ishmaelites were fighting for her possession."

ReDaK often quotes both Ibn Ezra and his own father, Joseph, to whom he refers as *My Master, my father, may his memory be for a blessing*. This is very fortunate, for in this way many of the interpretations of the senior Kimchi have been preserved for us. Of the latter's commentaries on the Torah, the Prophets, Proverbs and Job, only a few fragments have been preserved; while his other work, *Sefer HaBrit*, in which he refuted certain Christological interpretations of Scrip-tural verses, is again known to us only through references by his son David. For instance, in discussing Isaiah 7. 15, *ReDaK* says:

> "The answer to the heretics is explained in *Sefer HaBrit* which my master, my father, of blessed memory, com-posed in refutation of the heretics ..."[42]

It was, however, not only from his father and from Ibn Ezra that ReDaK acquired his understanding of the Bible record. His works are full of references and quotations from a wide range of sources, for he seems to have collected his

material from wherever he could find it; and, as is evident
from a number of his comments, he must have had an un-
usually large library for those days. On Judges 6. 19, for
instance, he refers to a *Compendium* (*Machberet*) *of Ben Asher*
and to certain other "books of reputed correctness" (*Sefarim
Meduyakim*). He drew extensively on talmudic and midrashic literature; and he names also authorities like Sa'adya
Gaon, Samuel HaNagid and Ibn Gabirol, whose literary
heritage was known to him in Arabic. On Psalms 132. 6, he
offers the explanations, in order, of Chiquitilla, his own
father, Ibn Ezra, the Midrash ("the words of our Sages");
and finally he says—"And it seems to me ..."—and proceeds to give his own interpretation. Indeed, one of his
chief characteristics is that he was a great collector of interpretations and outlooks of all Bible commentators who had
preceded him; and he presents, in a most lucid style, a
wealth of knowledge in almost every department of Jewish
learning—philology, grammar, midrash, law, philosophy.
Sometimes, having given a traditional rabbinic interpretation, he shows his disagreement with it, adding, "but according to the straightforward, literal sense, etc. ..." Nevertheless, he shows humility and modesty in the face of rabbinic tradition. A good illustration of this is his comment on
the episode of Jephtha and his daughter (see on Judges 11.
31). Following his father, *ReDaK* suggests that Jephtha fulfilled his vow not by literally sacrificing his daughter, but
by her being "given to the Lord"—i.e. by her not being
allowed to marry. "So it seems to me according to the plain
sense of the verses", he says; "but," he hastens to add, "if
it is a tradition (*Kabbala*) of the Sages (that Jephtha offered
up his daughter as a sacrifice) then we should accept it."[43]
  On the other hand there are some places where he adopts
a critical approach which is not easily to be reconciled with
his usual orthodox attitude. A typical case is his explanation

of the repetitions and parallisms in the Bible. He takes care to point out that his father saw in these repetitions some special significance—an extra meaning; as when Jeremiah declares: "Trust not in lying words, saying: The Temple of the Lord, the Temple of the Lord, the Temple of the Lord are these", which Joseph Kimchi explained as referring to "three parts"—the porch, the Temple proper, and the Holy of Holies." But *ReDaK* himself opposes this view, suggesting that the repetition is used by Scripture merely for the sake of emphasis (*LeChazek*). (See Finklestein's edition of *The Commentary of David Kimchi on Isaiah*, Introduction.)

Another, most significant, example is his treatment of the text where there is the *Keri* (i.e. the Massoretic text, as it is to be read) and the *Ketiv* (i.e. the marginal text, as it is written but not read). He invariably explains the two versions, and, in the Introduction to his commentary on Joshua, he sets out clearly the principle he follows:

> "These differences of reading occur because in the course of the first exile the books were lost, the scholars dispersed, and the students of the Torah died; so that the Men of the Great Synagogue, who restored the Torah to its previous status, found differences of reading among the manuscripts, and they accepted the reading of the majority according to what they thought best ... They accepted one reading for the main text, and put the other in the margin"—(Finkelstein, ibid.).[44]

On I Kings 17. 14, he repeats his view as follows:

> "In the course of the Dispersion, the texts became confused and one text was found to read thus and another otherwise. As it was impossible to decide which was correct, the one was adopted, and the variant placed in the margin"—(Ibid.).[45]

In this rather daring critical approach, the more scientific background of Spain seems to have prevailed over the more fundamentalist northern strain of the French talmudic schools.

If we bear in mind that R. David Kimchi only began to write when he was about forty years old, we shall see how assiduous he must have been in his subsequent teaching and literary labours. In the next thirty years, he wrote his Hebrew Grammar and Dictionary, followed by commentaries on Chronicles, the Early Prophets, the Later Prophets Psalms, and Genesis—as well as some other works. But these labours did not prevent him from taking an active interest in the life of his times. Firstly, he seems to have been very concerned to prevent the use of the Bible in support of Christian teaching, and he used every opportunity—especially when interpreting the Psalms—to attack Christian theology (see particularly Psalm 110). Secondly, within the Jewish camp, the big issue of the day was the conflict for and against Maimonides, which flared up with excessive zeal following Samuel Ibn Tibbon's translation into Hebrew of the *Guide*. When the northern French rabbis pronounced a ban against the *Guide* and the philosophic portions of the *Code*, the communities of Provence—and especially the scholars of Lunel and Narbonne—rose in protest; and R. David Kimchi, now advanced in years, was chosen as an emissary to go to Spain to win over the Spanish Jewish communities to the side of rationalism and tolerance. *ReDaK* took a vigorous stand in defence of the works of Maimonides against the anti-Maimunists. The fact that he was chosen to represent the Maimunist cause in Spain shows that his fame must have been well established in his own lifetime even beyond the borders of his native Provence.

As to the fame and popularity of his commentaries, it is sufficient to state that the *ReDaK* commentary on the

Psalms was one of the first Hebrew books published, and that his commentaries on the prophetic books were published even before the actual texts of the books themselves. Gradually, the older Arabic commentaries on which Kimchi had drawn so largely, were forgotten, and Kimchi was henceforth to rank with Rashi and Ibn Ezra as the standard Bible commentators.

12

Moses Nachmanides

MAIMONIDES, in whose life and work the summit of medieval Jewish philosophy was attained, died in 1204. His Code—or *Mishne Torah*—and, to a much greater extent, his *Guide to the Perplexed*, produced the rumblings of a conflict which was to break with full force only after his death, when the *Guide* became widely known through being translated into Hebrew (from the original Arabic) by Samuel Ibn Tibbon. It was then that the storm broke which split Jewry into the Maimunist and anti-Maimunist camps for a whole century. This (the thirteenth) century was the most eventful period of the Middle Ages. It was a period of intellectual expansion, and Maimonides was the distinguished forerunner of this pinnacle of medieval intellectualism. In the year of his death (1204) the capture of Constantinople by the Crusaders brought to Europe the full and original works of Aristotle which had until then been available only in part and in Arabic versions. Now classical and philosophical learning took a big step forward; but at the same time, there grew up a corresponding anti-philosophical reaction. Thus we find the Christian Church adopting an antagonistic attitude toward Aristotle and banning translations of his works for fear of the rise of heresies. So also were there rabbinic authorities who feared that the spread of philosophy among the Jews would lay waste their religious life—that the purity of Jewish thought and tradition might be sullied by foreign influences. They felt it necessary to preserve traditional

Judaism (*Kabbala*) from being encroached upon by secularist thinking (*Chochma*).

In this conflict between Jewish fundamentalists and "intellectualists", there stood, chiefly as mediator, the commanding figure of Moses Nachmanides, or, in Hebrew, *RaMbaN*—i.e. Rabbi Moses ben Nachman. Solomon Schechter has finely said that Nachmanides represented Judaism from the side of emotion and feeling, as Maimonides did from the side of reason and logic. Born in Gerona, in 1195, Nachmanides spent nearly the whole of his life in Christian Spain, and was the outstanding personality in Jewry and Jewish learning in the thirteenth century. Though in northern Spain, Gerona was very much under the influence of French Jewish scholarship, and Nachmanides drank deep at the fountain of the French Rabbis with their especial emphasis on talmudic learning and piety. By the time he reached the age of fifteen he had begun to write treatises and comments on the Talmud in the style of his French masters, the *Tosaphists*, or "Supplementers", as they were called; and it was through him that the study of the Talmud was raised to prime importance in Spain, just as it had always been in the north. At the same time, Nachmanides was not isolated from the influences of Spanish scholarship, and he was completely at home in the secular sciences. In fact, he earned his livelihood as a physician; and in him we find a harmony and synthesis between the piety, the veneration of earlier authorities, the unswerving acceptance of tradition and of the teachings of the early Sages as typified by the French schools on the one hand, and the love of secular learning in all its widest aspects, including philosophy and the natural sciences, characteristic of the Spanish background.

In the Maimonidean controversy, Nachmanides seems to have been puzzled as to which way to turn. He hesitates and temporises. He was impressed by the fact that the French

rabbis had proclaimed a ban (or *cherem*) against the *Guide*;
but at the same time he tried, though unsuccessfully, to
persuade the Spanish authorities not to issue a counter ban
against the anti-Maimunists. In the event, the northern
scholars not only decreed that the philosophical books of
Maimonides were heretical and dangerous, and must not
be read, but in their wrath they turned to the Church
authorities for help, and the books were condemned to be
burnt in Paris in 1232. Nachmanides tried continuously to
bring the opposing factions together. In a letter to the
French rabbis he stressed the virtues of Maimonides' work,
and pointed out particularly that the *Guide* had been
intended to help those Jews who were troubled by doubts to
reconcile their new philosophy with the old religious teachings. Nevertheless, he could not himself regard philosophy
as the touchstone of religious truth, and in this a huge gulf
separated him from Maimonides. To him the teachings of
Scripture and the Talmud were authoritative, no matter
which way reason might point. Whatever happens in the
world he accepts as the direct handiwork of God. He was
emphatically opposed to the rationalistic approach which
sets up the human intellect as judge in questions of Holy
Writ. At the very commencement of his commentary on
Genesis, he proclaims his guiding principle:

"Moses wrote this book, together with the whole of the
Torah, at the dictation of the Holy One, blessed be He;"[46]

and again,—

"It is true and clear that the whole of the Torah, from the
beginning of Genesis unto 'in the eyes of all Israel' (Deut.
34. 12) was given by the mouth of God to the ears of
Moses."[47]

He goes even further, in the spirit of the Kabbalists, and asserts:

"Everything (i.e. all knowledge) is either written plainly (in Scripture) or else is hinted at in the written words or in the computation of the numerical values of the letters, or in the shape of the letters;"[48]

"We further possess a true tradition that the whole of the Torah is made up of the Names of God."[49]

This new esoteric doctrine was soon to be formulated and proclaimed to the world as the *Kabbala* (or 'Tradition')—the approach of Jewish mysticism. Nachmanides was not a full-fledged Kabbalist, for he was still imbued with the scientific spirit and had much worldly learning, but his standing and authority gave a great push and encouragement to this new movement based on traditional mystic lore and called *Chochma Nistara*—"secret wisdom". What appealed to him was the fundamental conception that there must be a deeper meaning in the Scriptural word than appears on the surface in the literal sense. Thus while, on the one hand, he approached the Talmud with a keen dialectic mind, piercing every obscurity, on the other hand the mystic, emotional side of his nature and temperament found inspiration in the Kabbala.

Nachmanides lived a happy and busy life, teaching, writing, and practising medicine, surrounded by family and friends, and held in the highest esteem. We are told that his words were held in Catalonia in almost as high authority as the Scriptures themselves. But suddenly, all this tranquillity was upset. A convert to Christianity challenged him to a public disputation on the relative truths of Judaism and Christianity in the presence of the King and his Court. He was caught in a trap. If he should be worsted in debate, the

Jewish community would be forced into apostasy. But if he should win the argument, the populace might take revenge on the Jews in a more bloody form. Nachmanides distinguished himself; but his victory was almost too complete, as it drew on him the enmity of the Dominicans, and as a result he was condemned to exile. Accordingly, in 1263, in his seventieth year, he migrated to Palestine, where he spent his remaining years completing his Commentary on the Torah and reviving Jewish religious and communal life which had been almost extinguished by the Mongol invasion of a few years earlier. Here his emotional temperament showed itself in his great love for the Holy Land. "Even in this destruction it is a blessed land," he wrote in a moving letter to his children describing the ravaged condition of the country as well as his own sadness at being parted from his beloved family. And yet the letter is a strange mixture of sadness and hope, ending with the words:

"These are the words of your father who is yearning and forgetting, who is seeing and enjoying,
Moses ben Nachman."

This same mood is expressed in an appendix to his Torah-Commentary where again his nationalist fervour rises above his sense of exile and loneliness:—

"Oh, I am the man who saw affliction. I am banished from my table, far removed from friend and kinsman, and too long is the distance to meet again. ... But the loss of all else which delighted my eyes is compensated by my present joy in a day passed within thy Courts, O Jerusalem! ... Where it is granted me to caress thy stones, to fondle thy dust, and to weep over thy ruins. I wept bitterly, but I found joy in my heart. I rent my garments, but I found solace in doing so."

Nachmanides' two-sided inspiration, standing as he did on the border of France and Spain, is evidenced in his constant references to Rashi, representing the northern school, and to Ibn Ezra, the greatest Spanish Bible commentator. He quotes them over and over again, explaining them and arguing against them. In the Introduction to his own Commentary, he says:

> "I shall set up as the light of my countenance ... the commentaries of Rabbi Solomon (i.e. Rashi) ... He has pride of place. I shall pay heed to his words. ... I shall deal with them and enquire and search diligently into them. ... And we shall also show *open rebuke* and *hidden love* to Rabbi Abraham Ibn Ezra."

His references to Rashi are always in a spirit of greatest respect and deference. Although he sometimes differs from him, his arguments are presented like those of a student sitting at the feet of his master; and only rarely does he permit himself to use sharp language, as, for example, "there is neither taste nor fragrance in his explanation"—(Lev. 19. 16). There was however one aspect of Rashi that he disliked intensely, and that was Rashi's occasional explanation on the basis of non-Jewish usage. Thus, on Ex. 28. 41, Rashi explains the expression—"And thou shalt consecrate them" —with a reference to the Old French:

> "And in the O.F. language—when a person is appointed to a certain charge, the Prince puts into his hand a leathern glove which they call *gant* in O.F. ... and they term that transmission of the glove (and the office) *revestir* in O.F.";

but Nachmanides comments: "He (Rashi) adduces evidence from the fools!" The fundamentalist pietism in Nachmanides induced him to spurn such "foreign" explanations!

86

Vastly different was his attitude towards Ibn Ezra, the learned and worldly-wise Spaniard. Here there is nothing of the deference he shows to Rashi. Weiss, in his *Dor Dor Vedorshov*, has well remarked that *RaMbaN* amply fulfilled what he said about showing "open rebuke" to Ibn Ezra— "but where is his 'hidden love' (*Ahava Mesuteret*)?" he asks. When he agrees with Ibn Ezra's explanations, he does so tersely and almost grudgingly. *Yafe Piresh*—"He has explained well," is a comment often found (Ex. 29. 46 etc.); or *Ve Nachon Hu*—"He is right." On the other hand, when he disagrees with him he often attacks him sharply:

"Let not Rabbi Abraham lead you astray with his problem-questions"—(Gen. 11. 28).

"Behold R. Abraham has left his path in the plain simple explanations of the text and has begun to prophesy falsehoods"—(Gen. 9. 18).

Despite his usual pious and modest demeanour, Nachmanides becomes aggressive in his attitude towards Ibn Ezra, possibly because the latter was not famed as a Talmudist. Similarly Nachmanides refers frequently to the "true" inner understanding and knowledge of the meaning of the text as vouchsafed only to those who have entered into the mysteries of the Kabbala; and from this point of view, too, he regards himself as superior to the uninitiated Ibn Ezra and shows intolerance towards him. Thus, on Ex. 33. 12, he says of him: "Ibn Ezra has understood with his intellect ... but he cannot know the truth, for he has not heard it, nor can he prophesy." His tone is scornful towards his Spanish predecessor who was not blessed with this gift of "hidden wisdom"—(*Chochma Nisteret*, from whose initial letters the term *Chen* was coined). For the same reason his rejection of some of Maimonides' explanations was equally sharp. On Gen. 15. 2, there is a most severe comment on the *RaMbaM*:

> "These words contradict the Scriptural text; it is forbidden to hear them, let alone believe them."[50]

Nachmanides could not abide the purely rationalistic approach to Scripture. Divine teachings, he insisted, are beyond and above human comprehension, and are not subject to its limitations. Consequently, he set great store by the traditions transmitted by the ancient Sages in the midrashim and other rabbinic literature, and even in their words he senses often an inner "hidden" meaning. A phrase often used by him in summing up his comments is: *Hamaskil Yavin*—"And he who has discernment will understand;" and sometimes, when he has given a reasonable explanation according to the *Peshat*, he goes on: *Ubifnimiyut HaInyan*— "But the *inner* face, the real secret core, of the matter, is ..." (e.g. Gen. 1. 3). In this way, Nachmanides prepared the ground for the later Kabbalists, and one of them, Rabbi Bachaye b. Asher (d. 1340 C.E.), in his Torah-commentary, said of him: "He showed us the way we should go, and led us by the way of truth; he it was who merited us and sustained us".

Nevertheless, the spirit of worldly learning which characterised his Spanish background also found ample expression in his writings. Again and again, after quoting and expounding a midrashic explanation, he goes on to say: "But in my opinion the literal plain sense (*Peshat*) is ..." He also makes frequent use of the sciences, especially medical knowledge. And more than all other commentators, he diligently enquires into the connection between the chapters and portions of the Torah. To him, the juxtaposition of the portions is not fortuitous nor haphazard, but meaningful and pointed; and, in opposition to other teachers (including

Rashi), he maintains that there is a chronological sequence and order throughout Scripture, except where the text itself indicates a deviation from the chronological order.

RaMbaN's commentary to the Torah remains to this day one of the most important, just as his personality ranks among the most colourful in Jewish history.

13

Don Isaac Abravanel

THE AWFUL DECLINE in the condition of the Jews in Spain, which followed in the wake of advancing militant Christendom in that country, rushed headlong to its tragic climax in the fifteenth century. The wheel of fortune had turned. The shadow of the Christian Church fell across that sunny land where Jewish learning and literature had for centuries found a congenial home, where kings had been patrons of Hebrew poets and philosophers and where Jews had served loyally as statesmen and governmental advisers. "Baptism or death!" now became the watch-cry throughout the land; and the agonies of the cruel Inquisition, with the constant dread of informers, led eventually to the Edict of Expulsion in 1492. Of the estimated hundred and fifty thousand exiles, many were robbed and murdered at sea. Famine and brigands attacked those who reached North Africa. Many found temporary but very short-lived safety in Portugal, while others made their way to different parts of Christian Europe where again they were regarded as objects for religious conversion. The luckiest of them found their way to Italy, where the Popes and the States had for long left the Jews in peace. In particular, there was no central government, for Italy consisted of separate States, so that if circumstances became dangerous for the Jew in one State, there was always another, not far away, to which he could run for refuge.

Against this background of uncertainty and insecurity, there stands out the princely personality of Don Isaac Abravanel. Born in 1437 in Portugal, he quickly became

accustomed to the atmosphere of Court circles. For his
father was the King's Treasurer and used his position to give
Isaac an excellent secular education as well as having him
trained in Jewish matters by the Rabbi of Lisbon, Joseph
Hayyim. Isaac lived in Lisbon for the first forty four years of
his life, and later he referred to this period nostalgically as
the happiest in his life (v. commentary on Kings). He mixed
with the mighty in the land, and his home was a centre for
the learned—both Jews and non-Jews. Moreover, at an early
age, he began to write. His first book, *Ateret Zekenim*, was
composed when he was only twenty; and at this time he
also prepared the material for his commentary on Deuteronomy, but this was published only after an interval of
many years. His literary work was interrupted by the fact
that he was appointed to the King's service in succession to
his father, and thus he entered on his public career as Statesman and politician. In 1481, however, the King, Alphonso V,
died, and, as Abravanel wrote, "all Israel was filled with
grief and mourning: the people fasted and wept." Indeed,
they had cause to do so; for under the new king, the benign
protection they had enjoyed ceased. Abravanel himself was
accused of complicity in treason and, in 1483, had to flee to
Spain, where he settled in Toledo, a penniless refugee.

The next nine years constitute the middle period of his
life. His personal disaster did not completely overwhelm
him. On the contrary, he seems deliberately to have made a
virtue out of necessity. On arrival at Toledo, being now
freed from the yoke of the royal service, he immediately set
to work at full speed on his Biblical commentaries which he
had projected for some time. He was an amazingly fast
worker, for within six months he had completed lengthy
commentaries on the books of Joshua, Judges and Samuel. He
also began a commentary on Kings, but once again he was
forced by other duties to lay his pen aside. His fame had

gone before him, and now the King of Spain called him into his service. In this position he was able to use his influence a good deal on behalf of his brethren, protecting them from the horrors of the Inquisition. Even when the blow of expulsion fell, Abravanel did all in his power to induce the King to revoke the harsh edict. He offered large sums of gold to his Sovereign to ransom his people; but Torquemada, the apostate-Jew who had become the arch-inquisitor, cried out: "Judas sold his Master for thirty pieces of silver. Will your Majesties sell him now for thirty thousand ducats?"

Abravanel found protection in Naples, and, once again free of the cares of office, the first thing he did was to complete his commentary on Kings. But King Ferdinand of Naples had also heard of Abravanel's ability and quickly raised him to high office. Three years later, however, Naples was overrun and again Rabbi Isaac had to flee—this time to Sicily. The death of his patron here made it necessary for him to go to Corfu, and finally we find him settled in Venice, stricken with sorrows, his family scattered and his fortune gone, seeking consolation in his scholarly work and labouring over his commentaries until his death in 1509.

The most obvious feature of Abravanel's commentaries is the diffuse style of his writing. We have noted already that he always wrote in a hurry—when he was not otherwise engaged. But during all those years when his pen was still, he was constantly reading and thinking and preparing the material, so that as soon as the opportunity came he was able to write unhesitatingly. His preparation of much of this material was in the form of lectures which, it seems, he gave constantly. In the Introduction to his Commentary on Joshua he says:

"Behold the Lord God has chanced to bring to me here

learned and famed men, friends who listen to me. ... With them I hold conversation, and they listen to what I have to say. They have asked me to set my hand to explain the books of Joshua, Judges, Samuel and Kings."[51]

Again at the conclusion of Joshua he refers to his lectures in which he had expounded his views "night after night". So also at the end of Judges he says he has written down—

"What God put into my mouth at the time of my study with the friends who listened to my teaching."

In this way the Commentaries were formed in his mind, and all he had to do was to dash them off into writing. The result is that he is diffuse and verbose. He often repeats himself, and his language flows on without brake or hindrance. This makes his work somewhat difficult to read nowadays, but it is a natural and spontaneous style which must have greatly attracted the listeners to his lectures, as his son Judah testifies in a dedicatory poem:—

"Wise men stored up words before him, and they waited for his word as for dew."[52]

Abravanel is conscious of the fact that he is lengthy, but suggests that this is a virtue. In fact, he attacks other commentators who had preceded him—especially Rashi and Ibn Ezra—for their brevity which, he says, "indicates the brevity of their understanding of the truth of the verses..."

"Did they not know or understand that there are seventy meanings (faces) to the Torah? How, then, can they explain them in a few words? I am not like that, for whenever it is necessary to be lengthy, I have no right to be brief"—(Intro. to Joshua).[53]

In one passage, he jeers at Ibn Ezra, saying that "his explanation is shorter than the verse itself." While most other commentators tried to explain the text of each verse as they went, dealing with points of grammar and philology, giving the simple *Peshat* or superficial rational meaning, or adducing a *Midrash* to give a homiletical interpretation, Abravanel's commentaries read like long dissertations on the content of the passage as a whole—sometimes a whole chapter or book at a time.

The special distinctiveness, however, of his work, his really original contribution to the method of Scripture-commentary, is in his famous Introduction to each book. He prefaces each book with a general Introduction in which he not only gives a summary of its contents but also deals with such questions as the general character and purpose of the book, its author, and the date of its composition. Each book is then divided up into sections, and to each section he prefaces six general questions or problems (*She'elot*), and then proceeds to deal with them. He admits that the number six is arbitrary and artificial, but he says he has rigidly adhered to this pattern as an aid to memory. Nevertheless, in the five books of the Torah, the number of these "questions" to each of his "sections" is often much greater. Among these "questions" he raises many difficult problems, such as the use of the different names of God, the discrepancies between parallel accounts in Samuel and Kings on the one hand and Chronicles on the other; and this method affords him the opportunity to expound his views on numerous other topics, among them the relative merits of monarchy and republic (Deut. 17. 14; 1 Sam. 8); the meaning of *Edom* in the Bible (on Is. 34. 6) as being applicable to Christianity; the difference between Judges and Kings; the significance of sacrifices; the development of Hebrew poetry and its relation to Arabic poetry (on Ex. 15).

Opposed though he was to the rationalistic approach of
Maimonides and the other philosophers who sought to
explain miracles on a natural and scientific basis, it is yet
difficult to call him a fundamentalist. He was far removed
from the Kabbalists—

"For I have not learnt the wisdom of Kabbala, and I do
not possess the wisdom of the holy ones"—(Gen. 50);[54]

and again (Deut. 4. 19)—

"I have nothing to do with hidden things, and I have not
walked in the ways of the Kabbala—for that is far from
me."[55]

And his attitude to the midrashim of the talmudic Sages
was critical though respectful. In his introduction to Joshua,
he says:

"I shall use those midrashim and other sayings of the
Sages which appeal to me most. ... But I shall not restrain
myself from showing their weakness wherever their
words convey their own explanation and not their
accepted tradition."

Similarly, on Isaiah 23, he has this to say with regard to the
midrashic explanations:

"This does not seem reasonable to me. ... Therefore if it
is a tradition we have to accept it; but for the simple
meaning of the text, we should not move from what the
fact of the prophecy and its proofs will show."

Rashi, he felt, had stuck too closely to the homiletical interpretations of the Rabbis; but as for him, his method is to use
a midrash whenever he can show that it agrees with his own
interpretation. The result is that though he uses much
homiletical material, the general impression is of a rational

approach based on commonsense, general knowledge and experience. For instance, in the story of Rahab and the spies (Josh. 11. 1), the Targum translates the word *Zona* (harlot) as "inn-keeper"; and Abravanel adds the comment that the Targum does not suggest thereby that Rahab was not a harlot, but merely indicates that she practised her harlotry under the guise of an inn-keeper. Again, in the first chapter of Exodus, where the text speaks of the Hebrew midwives, Abravanel explains that it means: "the (Egyptian) midwives for the Hebrew women." For, he says, Pharaoh would surely not have been so foolish as to have appointed Hebrew women for this task! This commonsense, rational approach even leads him, sometimes, to suggest shortcomings and failings in revered figures of the Bible. Thus he notes that there are numerous marginal Massoretic notes (*keri* and *ketiv*) in Jeremiah, and this he attributes to the fact that Jeremiah was very young when he began to prophecy—

"and therefore was not, as yet, perfect in the use of the language,"[56]

so that corrections had to be made later on.

Abravanel was the first Jewish commentator to give consideration to social and political factors as a background for the understanding of the Bible. Here was a direct result of his own experience as a professional statesman who spent his life in consort with kings and international affairs. He continually draws on his own first-hand knowledge of these matters in seeking to explain Biblical laws or events. In connection with the coronation of Saul he discusses the relative merits of monarchy and republic, and illustrates his arguments with examples from ancient Rome and contemporary Italian states. Likewise, in his Introduction to

Judges, he compares the procedure for the crowning of the Kings of Israel with that for European kings.

Alas, his intimate association with political affairs brought home to him with greater force the weakness and tragedy of the position of the Jewish people. The dreadful events he lived through, and especially the horrors attendant upon the Expulsion from Spain, drove him to search for some explanation to the awful catastrophe, so that he might give a message of consolation and renewed faith to his suffering people. To this end he delved deeply into the Scriptural record, and wrote three Messianic works in which he urged that the Messiah was bound to come in their day. The first of these books he called *Ma'yene Hayeshu'a* (Wells of Salvation), in the Introduction to which he wrote:

> "I have heard many saying, Our bones are dried up, our hope is lost. ... Therefore I said in my heart, It is a time to act for the Lord, to strengthen the hands of the weak, to comfort those who stumble in exile ..."

In fact, this book is a Commentary on the Book of Daniel.

The second of these Messianic books is called *Yeshuot Meshicho* (The Salvations of His anointed) and is a collection of talmudical sayings concerning the coming of the Messiah. And the third, *Mashmi'a Yeshua* (Announcing Salvation) is a commentary on the messianic prophecies in the books of the prophets and the Psalms. He is at great pains, in these works, to refute the Christian messianic teachings which explained Redemption as coming to the world at large through Christianity, and not to the Jewish people specifically:

> "As if we are the poor and the outcast, so that we should receive only the evil from God, but not the good!"[57]

> "And this is an amazing thing. Every good prophecy they

explain for the Christians, and every bad prophecy they refer to Israel."[58]

With the death of Isaac Abravanel we mark the passing of a whole epoch in Jewish history. Spanish Jewry was no more. But his son Judah, known as Leone Ebreo (Judah the Hebrew), was to continue to bring lustre to the name of his family by his poetry and his contribution to the splendour of the Italian Renaissance.

14

Moses Mendelssohn

FOR THE JEWS, the Middle Ages stretched on right up until
the eighteenth century. In particular, one of the sad and
tragic aftermaths of the Expulsion from Spain was the
eventual confinement of the Jews in ghettos. This step came
as the result of the inter-play of forces which really had
nothing to do with Jews or Judaism, except in the most
indirect way. In the sixteenth century, Martin Luther began
his attacks on the Papacy, and so the movement known as
the Reformation was born. At first, Luther calculated that
an easement of the condition of the Jews would more
successfully lead to their conversion; but when he saw that
this was not the case, he turned against them with bitterness
and hatred. Moreover, the Church in Rome took steps to
launch the counter-Reformation, and, in a big effort to
safeguard the Christian World, decided to segregate the
Jews from it. Thus the Jews were to bear the brunt of the
attack on both sides. For the Popes, who had hitherto
shown tolerance towards them, now determined to suppress
them, and, in 1555, a Papal Bull was issued which forced the
Jews to live in ghettos, and to suffer various other indig-
nities. The ghetto henceforth became the pattern for Jewish
life through most of Europe for more than two hundred
years.

Being herded into the narrow confines of the walled and
locked ghettos in every city, excluded from public office,
forbidden entry to most trades and agriculture, forced into
mean occupations—all this had its effect on the bearing, the

character and the mind. The Jew, who had been so superior, so elegant, so intellectual and worldly-wise in the great days of Spain and Italy, became now, after two centuries of the "ghetto's plague", indifferent to his appearance and uncultured in his speech. The ghetto put an end to all free exchange of thought with the outside world, and so the Jews were driven in upon themselves, upon the study of the Torah and the Talmud. Indeed, in time they came to find their own resources all-satisfying, and they no longer wished to share in the civilisation of their enemies and persecutors.

Against this narrowness and subjugation there came about a sharp reaction and revolt in the eighteenth century. New ideas were stirring in Western Europe—ideas of liberty and equality; and here and there some noble individuals were to be found who applied these ideas even to Jews! The man who was most responsible for loosening the bonds which still bound the Jews, especially in German-speaking countries, was Moses Mendelssohn—sometimes referred to as "the third Moses", for with him there began a new era in Judaism. (The second Moses was Moses Maimonides, 1135–1204.) Born in Dessau in 1729, his father, a poor scribe who earned a scant living by copying Scrolls of the Torah, gave him a good Jewish education and sent him to be tutored by the rabbi of the town, David Frankel. This rabbi was a first-class scholar, and he not only taught his eager pupil the Bible and the Talmud, but also introduced him to the philosophical commentators—especially to the work of Maimonides. When, a few years later, Frankel was called to Berlin, young Mendelssohn followed him, and there, in the great metropolis, living in most severe material conditions, he continued to study with his beloved master, and, at the same time, in spite of the prohibition of the ghetto, he began secretly to reach out after the knowledge and learning of the wider world round about. He found a friend who taught him mathematics, and another who tutored him in Latin. From yet another teacher he learned French and German, and soon there awoke in him a love for good literature and, especially, a flair for the German language in all its refinement and richness. Without college or regular schooling, he educated himself, and his cultivated tastes—particularly his favourite study, philosophy—gradually drew him into contact with other young intellectuals. Thus, at the age of about twenty five, he was introduced to Gotthold Lessing, the great liberal German author of the day, who was not ashamed to associate with a Jew. Lessing, indeed, had already shown himself opposed to intolerance in his play *The Jews*. Now there began a life-long friendship between the two men, which was to have important consequences. Taking Mendelssohn as his model, Lessing wrote another play which he called *Nathan the Wise* and in which he portrayed the Jew as tolerant, broadminded, modest and peaceful, in contrast to the fanatical Christians of his drama. In this way, the author bravely faced the intolerance of his contemporaries, and demanded justice for the Jew. Undoubtedly this play must be reckoned as one of the most powerful factors leading to Jewish emancipation.

Lessing also introduced Mendelssohn to German literary circles, encouraged him to write, helped him to publish his work, and generally led him to lose some of the shyness and awkwardness of the ghetto in spite of his added difficulty that he was a hunch-back and stuttered. Soon even the court was eager to get to know "the young Hebrew who wrote in German". He came into contact with Frederick the Great (even daring to criticise some of the king's poems) and with academicians and other men of note. Honours poured in upon him, and he won the essay prize of the Berlin Academy of Sciences, gaining the victory over Immanuel Kant. Still, there were some whose intolerance was not so easily overcome. Against his nature and temperament, he was forced to reply to the provocation of a Christian minister of Zurich, called Lavater, who earnestly hoped to convert Mendelssohn and all Jews to Christianity. In the end, Lavater apologised; but other Christians took up the cry. Finally, Mendelssohn got a friend to translate into German the *Vindiciae Judaeorum* (or "Defence of the Jews") written by Manasse ben Israel a hundred years earlier in his pleading for the re-admission of the Jews into England. Mendelssohn himself wrote a powerful and eloquent preface in which he pleaded for tolerance, for freedom of thought, and for equality for all before the law. To this he added his celebrated work *Jerusalem*, in which he boldly urged the separation of Church and State, which would bring the possibility of the enjoyment of civic rights by Jew as well as Christian.

Mendelssohn's struggle for the political emancipation of the Jew, for his recognition as a citizen and for his equality before the law, began to reap results. The Emperor Joseph of Austria issued new laws in 1781 opening the door for Jews to learn arts, handicrafts, sciences and agriculture. Certain irksome taxes were removed, and the Jew was admitted to the Universities. There was still a long road to travel, but the Jewish question had been brought to the attention of scholars, princes and statesmen.

At the same time as he strove to break down the ghetto-walls from without, he was equally concerned with the other side of the problem, namely, inspiring the Jews themselves to make contact with the modern world of culture. In order to achieve this he wanted them to drop the Yiddish they always now spoke among themselves, and acquire instead the German language. Only then would the Germans really understand the qualities and character of the Jew and only then would the Jew appreciate the treasures of modern thought. Moreover, he felt that their preoccupa-

tion with Yiddish had also led them away from the knowledge of their own Hebrew heritage, while their devotion to
the Talmud and its commentaries and supercommentaries
had cut them off from the true understanding and apprecia-
tion of the Bible itself. Accordingly, he set to work—at first
only for his own children, later on for wider publication—
to translate the Pentateuch into German. In order to make it
attractive and readily available to Jews, he decided to have
the German translation printed in Hebrew characters which
were more familiar to them. With the help of some friends
and collaborators, notably the Hebraist and Jewish historian
Solomon Dubno and another great Hebraist Naftali
Hirsch Wessely, he also provided a commentary (or *Biur*)
in Hebrew. Mendelssohn's edition of the Torah in this form
is known to this day simply as *The Biur*. At the time of its
appearance its effect was enormous. Some rabbinic authorities plainly regarded it as dangerous and forbade their
followers to use it. The most notable of these opponents
was Rabbi Yechezkel Landau, of Prague, who enjoyed wide
authority. Nevertheless, young Jews everywhere seized
upon the *Biur*, often behind their master's back, and used it
as a means of learning German as well as in order to gain an
understanding of the Torah. It was not long before thous-
ands of Jews had mastered the German language and were
groping their way into a vast new literature and a new world
of life and thought. From now on, Jewish children were
taught to regard the Bible as part of a wider German education, so that they could be brought up as Jews and Germans
at the same time; and, in order to help this aim forward still
more, Mendelssohn organised in Berlin a Jewish school in
which secular subjects, including technical branches so as to
fit the pupils for a vocation, were taught side by side with
Bible and Talmud.

When Mendelssohn died in 1786, he had done much to

stir the conscience of the Christians in the direction of Jewish emancipation; and he had roused the Jews to new intellectual life, having regained for them so much of what they had lost during their long imprisonment in the ghetto. But the new opportunities brought with them new temptations; and many of Mendelssohn's disciples threw overboard their Jewish heritage entirely in their eagerness to make themselves completely equal with their surrounding world and take full advantage of the new opportunity which was to develop still further after the French Revolution. "Civic emancipation together with fidelity to Judaism" had been the programme of Mendelssohn; "to give to Caesar what is Caesar's and to God what is God's." "Adapt yourselves to the manners and the constitution of the country in which you have been placed," he wrote; "but hold fast also to the religion of your fathers! Carry both burdens as well as you can." (*Jerusalem*, pt. 2.) How far these two things could be made to go together is the question which has determined so largely the course of the modern phase of Jewish history to this day.

From the point of view of Bible commentary, Mendelssohn's work marks the opening of a new era. Until his time, Scripture exposition had always been Jewish in origin, in conception, in outlook; it was never borrowed from outside sources. The non-Jewish world had, indeed, several times influenced Jewish commentary (one has but to think of Philo and Sa'adya as two examples), but the two were always divided very clearly. In fact Christian interpretation had always been greatly dependent on Jewish Bible exposition, and Christians had learnt from Jewish scholars both the method and the content of their commentaries. It is true that some Jewish commentators (Rashi, for example) often quoted non-Jewish sources and ideas, but usually this was done in order to refute them, and in order to instruct the

Jewish reader how to reply to his Christian neighbour in religious controversies and debates. From the time of Mendelssohn and onwards we meet with a new and different approach. The tables are turned, and we find Christian Bible commentary exercising a strong influence on Jewish interpretation. It is this which has led Jewish Bible scholars to be so devoted to Bible criticism—a new science developed in the liberal atmosphere of the nineteenth century by German Jewish and non-Jewish teachers. This science has led to the separation of Bible commentary from religion and its establishment as a general secular study. A more radical change in the Jewish attitude to Scripture it would be hard to imagine. But the fact is that the last hundred and fifty years have witnessed a growing process of studying the Bible not as Holy Writ, not as the living word of the Living God, but as if it were some secular text that had come down to us from ancient times, from the earliest period of Hebrew history. If Mendelssohn could have foreseen this tendency as a result of the "freedom in doctrine" which he advocated, he would have been appalled.

15

Malbim. The Expression of the Ghetto

THE LAST of the great Jewish commentators of the Middle Ages was Don Isaac Abravanel. He stood as a bridge bestriding or joining two periods in European history. On the one hand he was witness to the horrors of the Inquisition and the autos-da-fé and the Expulsion from Spain; but on the other hand he also saw the stirrings of the Renaissance, the invention of printing, and the discovery of America. Medievalism was fading into modernity. Abravanel lived on the threshold of a new world. But there was to be a big discrepancy between Jewish and European history. In European history, the era of ignorance and superstition was giving way before the new era of the revival of learning and culture. For the Jews, the very opposite was the case; for Abravanel's time marked the end of the rule of the mind, of worldly wisdom and learning, and the beginning of the dark ages of the ghetto. What the persecutions and expulsions had failed to achieve was now to be largely accomplished by the ghetto; for this restricted physical existence, with its social and economic limitations, was also a form of spiritual imprisonment which repressed the Jew's soul and benumbed his intelligence. This spiritual decay is evidenced particularly in the field of Scripture commentary in the next few centuries of ghetto-life. In the course of the two hundred and fifty years from the commentary of Abravanel to the *Biur* of Mendelssohn, hardly a single Bible commentary of importance appeared. This is not to say that there was no activity at all in this field. But exposition of the Bible in this period was either Kabbalistic in approach, basing itself on numerical computations (*Gematriot*), allegorical allusions and the like, or else it was conducted on the lines of the *Pilpul* method familiar from the study of the Talmud.

The term *Pilpul* is derived from the word *Pilpel* which means, literally, to spice, or to season, and hence metaphorically it came to be used in the sense of "to dispute violently, or cleverly". Thus *pilpul* became the term denoting a method of talmudic study by disputation, by penetrating investigation and the drawing of conclusions. By this method, a word or expression would be investigated by comparing it with similar expressions in other verses in order to establish the correct or basic meaning. Above all, the *pilpul* method is never satisfied with the superficial sense, and is far removed from the simple *Peshat*. Through its process of comparisons and deductions it was a particularly useful instrument, in talmudic times, for the development of the traditional Oral Law which was handed down in the form of short injunctions and tersely worded rulings and precedents. The clever pilpulist who, by his ingenious deductions, always proved a new point out of the transmitted material, was called *Oker Harim*—"Uprooter of mountains" (*Ber.* 64a); for so sharp was his reasoning that he could prove almost anything. And the cut and thrust of debate, which characterises so much of the Talmud, is based almost entirely on this method. After the close of the Talmud, the Geonim and early commentators concerned themselves chiefly with the arrangement of the text and its explanation, and some of them plainly indicated their displeasure where they thought the *pilpul* had been too acute and hair-splitting. Rashi, for example, says in his comment on one such passage (*Hullin* 81a):

"This is a wrong (false) explanation by one who is over-sharp and too steeped in *Pilpul*."[59]

Nevertheless this method gained ground, at first at the hands of the Tosaphists, and again from about the sixteenth century on, when it became the vogue mainly in Poland. From now on, the *pilpul* brought to the study of the Talmud the great shortcoming of concentrating more on the clever juggling and interpretation of the text than on its halachic or legal results. Most prominent rabbis of East Europe in the eighteenth and nineteenth centuries cultivated the *pilpul* style, and their fame was often built on their facility for hair-splitting dialectics and critical analysis. A marked degeneration set in in the use that was made of the pilpulistic method; for it was no longer regarded as a careful means of arriving at the correct sense of a given talmudic passage or of determining whether a particular ruling was sound. Instead it became looked upon as an end in itself, as a display of cleverness rather than a means of investigating the truth; and this was justified on the grounds that it was a means of sharpening the minds of the pupils in the Yeshivot and that it led them to think clearly and independently.

No doubt this rather introverted intellectualism was forced upon those generations by their ghetto conditions which cut them off from the outside world and denied them access to other scholarly interests. The evil effects of those conditions were felt to a particularly high degree in the East Europe of the nineteenth century. The progressive emancipation of the Jews in other parts of Europe, from the time of Mendelssohn to the seating of Rothschild in the English House of Commons in 1858, tended to build up a mark of division between them and Polish and Russian Jewry. Despite the liberal constitution of Poland of 1815, the Jews were still segregated from public life; and in 1827, under Czar Nicholas I, a special Statute was enacted concerning the Jews, heaping humiliations and restrictions upon them. It was this statute which laid down among other things, that

Jews could reside only in a limited Pale of Settlement, and that all Hebrew publications were to be subject to strict censorship. In these circumstances, the vast majority of Jews were afraid to peep out beyond the confines of their ghettos and the folios of their Talmud; and the *pilpul* method was not only a form of study for them, but also a principal means of relaxation and playfulness.

Though most of their attention was devoted to the Talmud, it was natural that they applied the same accustomed *pilpul* method in their exposition of the Scriptures. The sons of the ghetto brought the Bible down to the level of their own life and conditions and mode of thought; and they sought to explain it in terms of the halachic reasoning and rulings which were the stuff of their everyday preoccupations. Thus they reversed the process. Instead of deducing the halacha from the Bible-text, they read the rabbinic teachings into Scripture, and often Biblical characters were made the mouthpiece of those teachings.

The most outstanding and typical example of this ghetto-period in Biblical interpretation was Rabbi Meir Loeb ben Yechiel Michael (*Malbim*) who died at Kiev in 1879 after an eventful career which included the Chief Rabbinate of Bucharest and a period of imprisonment there, from which he was liberated through the intervention of Sir Moses Montefiore. His commentaries are known popularly as *The Malbim*, this family-name having been derived from the initials of his Hebrew name. Malbim's exposition is a mixture of Halacha and Aggada, of snippets of Kabbalistic mysticism, philosophic thought, and moralist (or *Musar*) sermons; but all is presented in the *pilpul* style. Yet he sincerely thought that he was expounding the Scriptures according to the plain and simple *Peshat*. Thus, in his Introduction to Joshua, he complains that most earlier commentators, with the exception of Abravanel, followed the method of homily (*Derash*),—but he steers clear of this approach:

> "I turned to the commentators ... but none of them bestirs himself to breathe the breath of life into the text according to the *Peshat*, except the Prince Isaac Abravanel and his band. ... For the other commentators turn only to *Derash*—with which we have nothing to do."

But as a matter of fact, Malbim did not recognise the difference between *Peshat* and *Derash*, and his explanations are far removed from the simple straightforward sense of the text.

Although the content of his material reflects the views of innumerable other earlier commentators, he appears to have admired particularly Abravanel, for he follows his method also in the presentation of his comments. Thus, like Abravanel, he prefaces each section with several questions or problems and then proceeds to explain them; the difference being that Malbim is not content with only six such questions (as was Abravanel) but posits many more, and puts them at the head of paragraphs and even of verses. But it is in his pilpulistic approach, putting halachic discussions into the mouths of Biblical personages, that he really typifies his time. For example, he explains the passage in Genesis where Sarah asks Abraham to send Hagar away as though Abraham had a discussion with Sarah on the legal point of whether a husband is permitted to free a maid-servant whom his wife brought as part of her dowry. Similarly, on Genesis chapter 37, where Joseph's "coat of many colours" is brought back to his father Jacob as evidence of Joseph's death, Malbim interprets verse 34 as follows: "And Jacob tore his garments"—*MiDin Avel*—"that was because of the law of the mourner;" "And he put sackcloth upon his loins"—

"that was as a sign of his repentance, as it is written in a certain responsa collection that if one sends a messenger to a place of danger and he is killed, he (the sender) has to do repentance."[60]

Another illustration of the pilpul style is Malbim's comment on the tragic vow of Jephtha that he would sacrifice the first thing that came out of his house to greet him, after his victory in battle, and the fact that the victim turned out to be his daughter. Malbim represents the situation as if Jephtha and his daughter, at that awful moment, had a legal discussion on whether his vow could be annulled by a rabbinical court:

"Jephtha held that there was a possibility of going back on his vow, but his daughter maintained there was no such possibility, and that a rabbinical authority had no power to uproot the vow …"[61]

Jephtha accepted his daughter's view; but, adds Malbim, the decision was wrong, for, according to the law, it *is* possible to annul a vow albeit not retroactively.

Such commentary seems unreal to us today. It seems to reduce the exposition almost to absurdity. But here we are witness to the tragic effects of the ghetto. Here also were the seeds of the subsequent reaction to the Yeshivot and to this type of talmudic learning, a reaction which burst forth towards the close of the century, in the movement known as the *Haskala* (Enlightenment)—with Jewish nationalism and the revival of the Hebrew language as its central themes.

16

Summing Up

IN THE PREFACE to his edition of Genesis (London, 1929) the late Chief Rabbi Dr. J. H. Hertz wrote: "The exposition of the plain, natural sense of the Sacred Text must remain the first and foremost aim in a Jewish commentary. But this is not its only purpose and function. The greatest care must be taken not to lose sight of the allegorical teaching and larger meaning of the Scriptural narrative; of its application to the everyday problems of human existence; as well as of its eternal power in the life of Israel and Humanity. In this way alone can the commentator hope not merely to increase the knowledge of the reader, but to deepen his Faith in God, the Torah and Israel."

In this description, Dr. Hertz has touched on the fundamental purpose and character of Jewish Biblical commentary. For, to the traditional Jew, the Bible is a book of revelation. The Torah is the law of God as He taught it to Moses on Sinai. It is eternal and unchangeable. Every sentence, every word of the Bible has its inner meaning and its message to teach. Therefore the Jew always accepted the Bible as the supreme and unquestioned authority in religious life, and every interpretation has been based on its sanctions. In every age since the close of Bible times, Jews have been united in the judgment of the Sage of the first century (in *Pirke Avot* 5. 25):

> "Turn it over and turn it over again, for everything is in it; study it and grow old in it, for thou canst have no better rule than this."

It is this attitude which basically accounts for the enormous amount of Biblical commentary material which has accumulated down the centuries. In contrast to Bible criticism, which assumes the right to amend the text and to analyse the various books of the Bible according to date, place and authorship, Biblical exegesis (or commentary) has accepted the traditional text and the traditional teaching as to authorship and similar questions, and has striven to explain the words of the text or to derive from them moral teachings.

Primarily, the Bible, for the Jew, always meant the code of religious law, the basis for religious teachings, the guide to morality and the embodiment of theology. It also is the first source-material available for a period of at least a thousand years in the history of the Jewish people; but it is only in modern times that the historical sense, as it were, seems to have been developed among Bible commentators, mainly under the impetus of the new movement of the nineteenth century, known as *Jüdische Wissenschaft*—("Jewish scientific learning"). Most earlier commentators were more concerned with the interpretation of the text as if it were almost a contemporary document, seeking to understand its moral and religious purpose. Among the earliest rabbinical authorities the maxim *En Mukdam Um'uchar Ba Torah*—"There is not necessarily any chronological sequence in the records of the Torah"—was adopted. Accordingly, the commentators surrounded the Biblical text with a wealth of notes to answer every question in the field of theology, ethics and natural law. Any knowledge which they derived from other, secular, sources, obtained added significance in their eyes when they were able to discover some indication of it in the Scriptures. Consequently, in studying the Bible, Jewish teachers were, consciously or unconsciously, always on the look-out to find in it support for information that was already in their minds. This "reading-in" process was especially carried to great lengths by the Rabbis of the Talmud and the early midrashic schools for *homiletical* purposes. It is true that they laid down the rule, *En Mikra Yotze Mide Peshuto*—that no interpretation was admissible which was incompatible with the *peshat* or plain meaning of the text. But in practice they paid little regard to this rule; or perhaps it would be more true to say that they thought they were adhering to the rule but that they were inevitably and unconsciously influenced in their respective appreciations of the *peshat* by the events and cultures of the times in which they each lived. The Scribes were concerned to guard the earliest records and to separate the holy books from those of lesser worth, and thus they led to the fixing of the Canon. Later it was necessary to bring comfort and hope to the generations who were brought to the brink of despair by the destruction of the Second Temple and the Second Commonwealth; and this resulted in midrashic teachings of the after-life, of the resurrection of the people of Israel, of the Messiah and the triumph of good over evil, and, above all, the eternity of the Torah and Israel. The rise of Christianity with its cry, "Believe and thou shalt be saved", produced the Jewish reaction of—*Lo Hamidrash HaIkar Ela Hama'ase*

"The principle thing is not study but *practice*",

laying the emphasis on the *Mitzvot Ma'asiyot*, the practical commandments, as the requirement of the Torah. Greek Hellenic culture produced the Septuagint, and a school of Jewish allegorical interpretation of the Bible with Philo as the leading and extreme exponent. Aristotelian philosophy affected all the early mediaeval Jewish scholars in their attitude to religion and the Scriptures and was responsible for so much of the work of Maimonides. The Arab conquests and the spread of Islam produced the Jewish reaction in the work of Sa'adya Gaon and the Spanish Jewish school covering the richest and most glorious period of Jewish life and letters in the post-Biblical era. So, also, the resurgence of a harsh militant crusading Christianity, the Reformation and the Renaissance, the dark ages of the Ghetto and the emergence to the new Enlightenment in the eighteenth and nineteenth centuries—all, all constituted a challenge and an influence, and all produced a reaction, within the Jewish people itself, which showed itself, first and foremost, in the attitude towards Bible interpretation.

There is one feature, however, which is common and constant through the entire field of Jewish Biblical commentary right up until the last century. This common denominator, axiomatically accepted by all, is the basic concept of the *unity of the Torah* and *its divine origin*. Nothing has so contributed to the preservation of the ancient text through the vicissitudes of Jewish history as this religious attitude. It was only in the nineteenth century, after the time of Mendelssohn, that Jews, finding their way to German universities, began to be influenced by the new "science" of Biblical criticism as it was then being developed by Christian Bible scholars. At the same time, the practice was begun of writing their critical commentaries in the German language so that they would not only reach Jewish readers, but would also be a contribution to the over-all German activity in this field and perhaps succeed in correcting some of the extremist Christian points of view. Unfortunately, through forsaking the Hebrew language, the link with the past, and with the two-thousand-year-old tradition of Jewish Scripture exposition, was severed. Discussion began to centre round purely *objective* issues—authorship, date of composition, suggested emendations of the text, and the like; and Biblical commentary, which had always been for the Jew an expression of religious love for a precious sacred heritage and an earnest searching after the Divine intention in and behind the unalterable words,—this long religious tradition was now changed into a *secular* science. Many of the assertions of the German so-called "Higher" Biblical Criticism have since been swept away by archaeological finds in the Middle East. But the tendency towards treating the Bible as a secular study still persists in some scholarly quarters. No doubt this is symptomatic, and perhaps in some degree a contributory cause, of the general unhappy secularisation of our age. The hope for the future lies in the fact that the millions of laymen and women who read the Bible today, Jew and Christian alike, do so not for its historical or archaeological interest, but chiefly in order to satisfy a subjective *spiritual* need. This was the main aim, and here is the permanent importance, of the Jewish traditional commentators.

1. ויקראו בספר בתורת האלהים מפרש ושם שכל ויבינו במקרא·

2. כי עזרא הכין לבבו לדרוש את תורת ד׳ ולעשות וללמד בישראל חק ומשפט·

3. שלמה יהיה שמו ושלום ושקט אתן על ישראל בימיו·

4. אנשי כנסת הגדולה·

5. אמר ר׳ ירמיה ואיתימא רבי חייא בר אבא תרגום של תורה אונקלוס הגר אמרו מפי ר׳ אליעזר ורבי יהושוע·

6. מי הוא זה שגילה סתרי לבני אדם? עמד עוזיאל בן יונתן על רגליו ואמר אני הוא שגיליתי סתריך לבני אדם· גלוי וידוע לפניך שלא לכבודי עשיתי ולא לכבוד בית אבא אלא לכבודך עשיתי שלא ירבו מחלוקת בישראל· ועוד בקש לגלות תרגום של כתובים יצתה בת קול ואמרה לו דייך· מ״ט משום דאית ביה קיץ משיח (מג׳ ג׳)·

7. כיוצאי דרכים·

8. ואיתגלי ד׳ לאתפרעא על עובדי קרתא·

9. גברין גברין בארע תותבותהון·

10. אומרים צדוקים, קובלים אנו עליכם פרושים שאתם אומרים כתבי הקודש מטמאין את הידים, ספרי המירס אינם מטמאין את הידים·

11. כתבי הקודש לפי חבתן היא טומאתן· ספרי המירס שאינן חביבין אי מטמאין את הידים·

12. משמתו חגי זכריה ומלאכי נסתלקה רוח הקדש מישראל·

13. אמר ר׳ שמעון בן עזאי מקובל אני מפי ע׳׳ב זקנים, ביום שהושיבו את ראב״ע בישיבה, ששיר השירים וקוהלת מטמאין את הידים· אמר ר׳ עקיבא חס ושלום לא נחלק אדם מישראל על שיר השירים שלא תטמא את הידים, שאין כל העולם כולו כדאי כיום שניתן בו שיר השירים לישראל, שכל הכתובים קודש ושיר השירים קדש קדשים· ואם נחלקו לא נחלקו אלא על קהלת·

14. זו משנה ר״ע· אבל משנה ראשונה···

15. זו משנה ראשונה· בית דין שלאחריהם אמרו···

16. סתם מתני׳ ר׳ מאיר· סתם תוספתא ר׳ נחמיה, סתם ספרא רבי יהודה, סתם ספרי ר״ש· וכולריו אליבא דר״ע·

17. ת״ר ארבעה נכנסו לפרדס ואלו הן בן עזאי ובן זומא אחר ורבי עקיבא···בן עזאי הציץ ומת···בן זומא הציץ ונפגע···אחר קיצץ בנטיעות ורבי עקיבא יצא בשלום·

18. וכי מפני שאתה דורש בת ובת נוציא זו לשרפה?

19. הרי אתה אומר לכתוב שתוק עד שאדרוש·

20. הלכה היא בידוע שעשו שונא ליעקב, אלא שנמכרו רחמיו באותה שעה ונשקו בכל לבו·

21. מפני כבודו של משה לשנות השם לומר שלא היה מנשה אלא משה (רש״י, רד״ק, וכו׳)·

22. חפישו באורייתא שפיר·

23. רוצים בו האור ההוא שנקרא שכינה (מ״ב פ״ח)·

24. רוצה בזה שהוא כאש שורף למי שכפר וכחש· ואני מוצא בלשון שהוא מדמה בלא כ״ף· ״ויוציא אתכם מכור הברזל״ שענינו כמכור הברזל···כן אש אוכלה עינו כאש אוכלה הוא, שהוא עונש (מ״ב, פ״ט)·

25. הדם הוא משכנה ומרכזה···וכשהיא שמחה ותראה שמחתה בדבר אשר תשמח בו, תראה הדם עמה, וכאשר תגוס מיראת דבר שתירא ממנו תקחהו עמה לפנים· ומה שאמרה התורה כי הדם הוא הנפש הוא על מנהג הלשון שהיא קוראה הדבר בשם משכנו· כאשר קוראה החכמה ״לב״ באמרה (משלי ז׳ ז׳) ״נער חסר לב״ מפני שהלב משכנה ···

26. שהמה מאירים השכל ומחדדים הבינה·

27. חלילה לאל שתבא בתורה במה שידחה ראיה או מופת‏·

28. היא ענין אלקי לא מן השכלי ולא מן הנפשי ולא מן הטבעי‏·

29. מדרגת עין והשקפת שכל לא השקפת עין‏·

30. המקום הרמוז עליו מן ההר אשר בו היה ההתבודדות והשגת השלמות‏·

31. ואבותינו פירש, מה שפירשו···אך אין סדר הפרשה והלשון מתישב בו‏

32. ואף אני··· נתווכחתי עמו לפניו והודה לי שאילו היה לו פנאי היה צריך לעשות פרושים אחרים לפי הפשטות המתחדשים בכל יום‏·

33. ואין תועלת לפרוש זה כי אם אורך (הקדמת אבן עז' לתורה)‏·

34. והרוצה לעמוד על חכמות החיצונות ילמדם מספרי אנשי תבונות (שם)‏·

35. כי אין הפרש בין שתי התורות ומידי אבותינו שתיהן לנו מסורות (שם)‏·

36. כי אם גם תורה שבכתב מיד אבותינו קיבלנוה וככה תורה שבעל פה מפיהם שמענוה‏· ואם אין אמת תורה שבעל פה הנה גם לתורה שבכתב אין מרפא (שם)‏·

37. וכל אלה דברי תהו הבל נדף ואין כמהו (שם)‏·

38. לזכר ואסמכתא בעלמא,

והם ידעו הפשט כי להם נתנה כל חכמה (שם)‏·

39. ומהשם לבדו אירא ולא אשא פנים לתורה (שם)‏·

40. אמר בן זוטא כי רעהו תואר לשור··· ואין לשור רע רק בן זוטא לבדו‏·

41. ובן לברט אמר כי אדדם כפול כמו אדום, ומי יתן וידום‏·

42. ולהשיב למינים בזאת הפרשה מבואר <u>בספר הברית</u> שחיבר א″א ז″ל בתשובת המינים···ושאר התשובות מסודרות שם <u>בספר הברית</u>‏·

43. דעת רז″ל בזה ידוע וא″א ז″ל פירש והעליתיהו הוי″ו במקום או··· ויפה פירש··· כי פרושה היתה, וזהו את נדרו אשר נדר‏· כך נראה לפי פשטי הפסוקים⁀ודברי רז″ל אם קבלה היא בידם עלינו לקבלה‏·

44. גם אכתוב טעם כתיב וקרי‪...‬ונראה כי המלות האלה נמצאו כן לפי
שבגלות ראשונה אבדו הספרים ונטלטלו החכמים ויודעי התורה מתו,
ואנשי כנסת הגדולה שהחזירו עטרה לישנה מצאו מחלוקת בספרים
והלכו בהם אחר הרוב לפי דעתם, ובמקום שלא השיגה דעתם על
הברור כתבו האחד ולא נקרא או כתבו מבחוץ ולא כתבו מבפנים וכן
כתבו בדרך אחד מבפנים ובדרך אחד מבחוץ‪.‬

45. וכבר כתבנו דעתנו בכתוב וקרי כי בגלות נשתבשו הנסחאות והיו
מוציאין (צ״ל מוצאין) בנסחא אחת כך ובנסחא אחרת כך ולא עמדו
על בירורם וכתבו האחת מבפנים והאחרת מבחוץ‪.‬

46 . משה כתב הספר הזה עם כל התורה כולה מפיו של הקב״ה‪.‬

47. אמת וברור הוא שכל התורה מתחלת ספר בראשית עד לעיני כל
ישראל מפיו של הקב״ה לאזניו של משה‪.‬

48. הכל נכתב בפרוש או שרמוזה בתיבות או בגימטריאות או בצורת
האותיות‪.‬

49. עוד יש בידינו קבלה של אמת כי כל התורה כולה שמותיו של הקב״ה‪.‬

50. ואלה הדברים סותרים הכתוב, אסור לשמועם אף כי להאמין בהם‪.‬

51. הנה פה הקרה ד׳ אלקים לפני אנשים חכמים וידועים חברים מקשיבים
לקולי‪...‬עמהם כל היום היא שיחתי ומאשר לי שמעו‪...‬ויבקשו
ממני לשלוח יד לפרש ספרי יהושע ושופטים שמואל ומלכים‪.‬

52. חכמים עצרו מלים לפניו
ויחלו כמטר אל דבריו‪.‬

53. הלא ידעו אם לא יבינו שיש שבעים פנים לתורה‪...‬ואיך יפרשום
במלות מועטות‪.‬ לא כן אנכי שבמקום שראוי להאריך איני רשאי
לקצר‪.‬

54. כי לא למדתי חכמת הקבלה ודעת קדושים לא אדע‪.‬

55. אין לי עסק בנסתרות ובדרכי הקבלה לא הלכתי, והיא רחוקה ממני‪.‬

56. ולכן לא היה עדיין שלם בדרכי הלשון ...

57. כאילו אנחנו חעניים והאביונים· את הרע נקבל מאת האלקים ואת הטוב לא נקבל·

58. וזה דבר נפלא כי כל נבואה טובה יפרשוה על הנוצרים ונבואה רעה יפרשוה על ישראל ...

59. פירוש משובש הוא מאדם חריף ומפולפלי·

60. לתשובה כמו שכתוב בשאלות ותשובות מהרי"ן שהשולח שליח במקום סכנה ונהרג חייב לקבל תשובה·

61. יפתח טען שיש פתח חרטה לנדרו והבת טענה שאין פתח חרטה לנדרו, ואי החכם יכול לעקור את הנדר מעיקרו·

WORKS CONSULTED AND RECOMMENDED FOR FURTHER STUDY

The following list of books is not presented as a complete Bibliography. It gives only a selection, in alphabetical order, of readily available works which the general reader, wishing to follow up the subject, may find useful.

ABRAHAMS, I. *Jewish Life in the Middle Ages*, 2nd Ed., 1932.

ABRAVANEL, ISAAC. *Six Lectures*, Ed. by J. B. Trend and H. M. Loewe, Cambridge, 1937.

Babylonian Talmud.

BACHER, W. Article on "Bible Exegesis" in *The Jewish Encyclopaedia*.

BOSNIAK, JACOB. *The Commentary of David Kimhi on the Fifth Book of the Psalms*, New York, 1954.

CHAJES, Z. H. *The Students Guide Through the Talmud.* Translated and edited by Jacob Schachter, 1952.

FINKELSTEIN, LOUIS. 1. *The Pharisees*, Jewish Publication Society of America, 1946.
2. *The Commentary of David Kimhi on Isaiah*, New York, 1926.

GASTER, M. *The Tittled Bible, a Model Codex of the Pentateuch: a Dissertation on the History of Tittles, their Origin, Date and Significance*, London, 1929.

GINZBERG, L. *Students, Scholars and Saints*, Jewish Publication Society of America, 1928.

GRAETZ, H. *History of the Jews*, English Ed., London, 1907.

HERFORD, R. TRAVERS. *Pharisaism*, London, 1912.

HERTZ, J. H., Chief Rabbi. *The Pentateuch and Haftorahs*, London, 1929–36.

HUSIK, Isaac. *A History of Mediaeval Jewish Philosophy*, 6th Ed., Jewish Publication Society of America, 1948.

Jewish Encyclopaedia, The.

LIBER, Maurice. *Rashi*, Jewish Publication Society of America, 1906.

MALTER, H. *Sa'adya Gaon, Life and Works.*

MARGOLIS, Max. *Hebrew Scriptures in the Making*, Jewish Publication Society of America, 1948.

MARGOLIS, M. and MARX, A. *History of the Jewish People*, Jewish Publication Society of America, 1927.

NETANYAHU, B. *Don Isaac Abravanel, Statesman and Philosopher*, Jewish Publication Society of America, 1953.

Rashi Anniversary Volume; Texts and Studies I, American Academy for Jewish Research, 1941.

ROBERTSON, E. *The Text of the O.T. and the Methods of Textual Criticism*, London, 1939.

ROSENBAUM and SILBERMANN. *Pentateuch With Rashi's Commentary*. Translated into English, London, 1929.

ROTH, C. *A Short History of the Jewish People*, East and West Library, Oxford, 1943.

RYLE, H. E. *The Canon of the Old Testament*, London, 1909.

SARACHEK, Joseph. *Faith and Reason: The Conflict over the Rationalism of Maimonides*, Williamsport, Pa., 1935.

SHACHTER, Jacob. *The Student's Guide Through the Talmud*, by Z. H. Chajes. Translated and edited by Jacob Schachter 1952.

SILVERSTONE, A. E. *Aquila and Onkelos*, Manchester University Press, 1931.

WAXMAN, M. *A History of Jewish Literature*, 1930–33.

WEISS, Isaac Hirsch. *Dor Dor VeDorshav* (Hebrew), 1876.

YELLIN, D. and ABRAHAMS, I. *Maimonides*, 1908.

Index